FOR ORGANS, PIANOS & ELECTRONIC KEYBOARDS

E-Z PLAY TODAY

151

BEACH BOYS
GREATEST HITS

T0045012

ISBN 978-0-634-03242-4

HAL•LEONARD®
CORPORATION

7777 W. BLUEMOUND RD. P.O. BOX 13819 MILWAUKEE, WI 53213

Visit Hal Leonard Online at
www.halleonard.com

Be True to Your School

Registration 7
Rhythm: Rock

Words and Music by Brian Wilson
and Mike Love

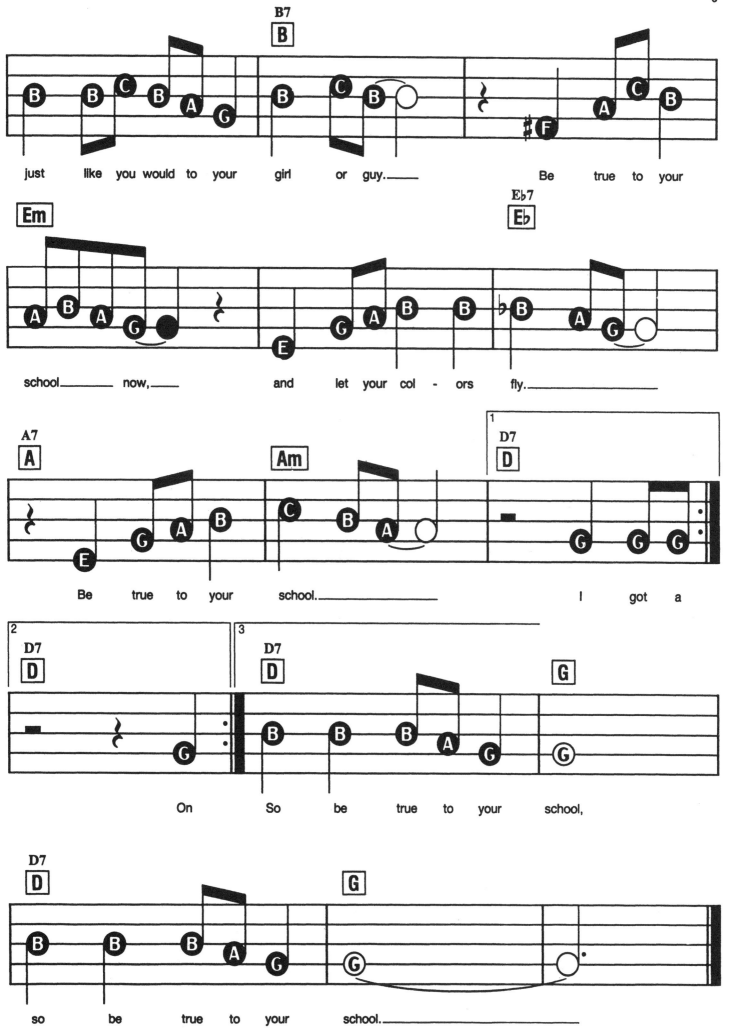

Barbara Ann

Registration 7
Rhythm: Rock

Words and Music by
Fred Fassert

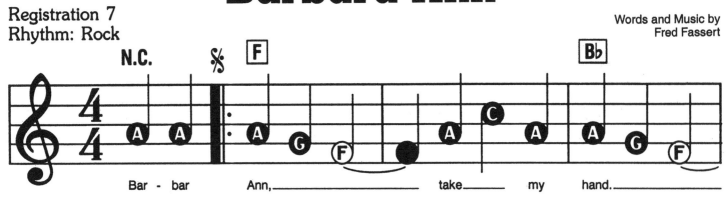

Bar - bar Ann, _____ take _____ my hand. _____

_____ Bar - bar Ann, _____ you got me

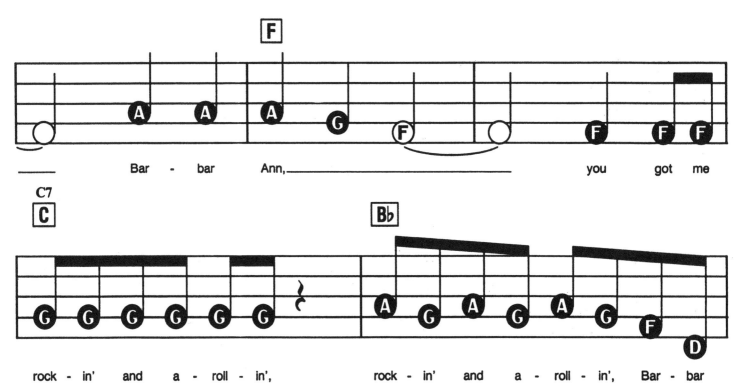

rock - in' and a - roll - in', rock - in' and a - roll - in', Bar - bar

Ann, Bar - bar - bar bar-bar Ann.

{ Went to a dance,
{ Played my fav - 'rite tune,

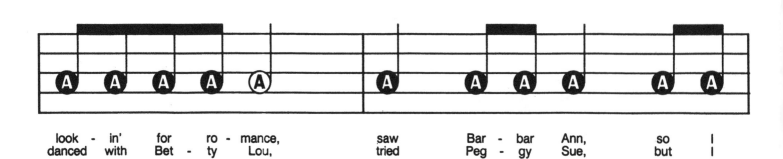

look - in' for ro - mance, saw Bar - bar Ann, so I
danced with Bet - ty Lou, tried Peg - gy Sue, but I

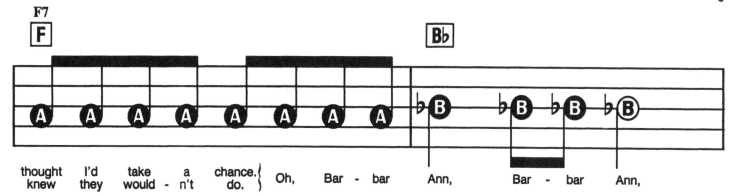

thought I'd take a chance. Oh, Bar - bar Ann, Bar - bar Ann,
knew they would - n't do.

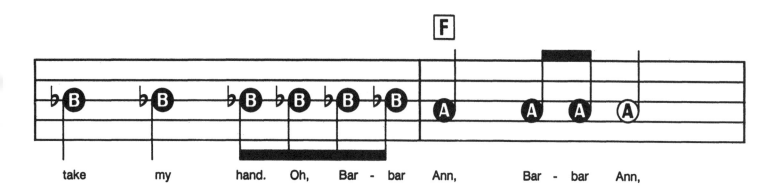

take my hand. Oh, Bar - bar Ann, Bar - bar Ann,

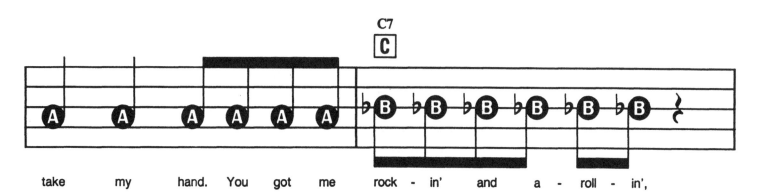

take my hand. You got me rock - in' and a - roll - in',

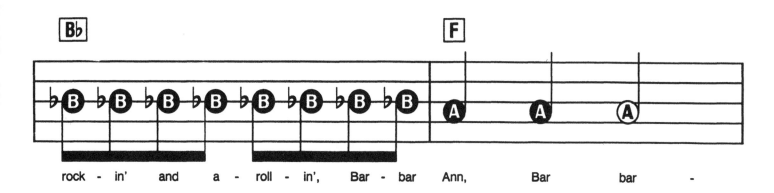

rock - in' and a - roll - in', Bar - bar Ann, Bar bar -

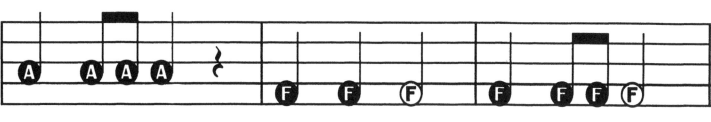

bar - bar-bar Ann. Bar - bar Ann, Bar - bar-bar Ann,

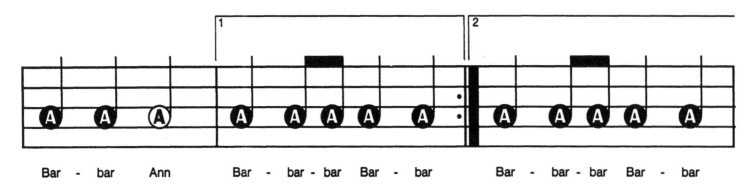

Bar - bar Ann   Bar - bar-bar Bar - bar   Bar - bar-bar Bar - bar

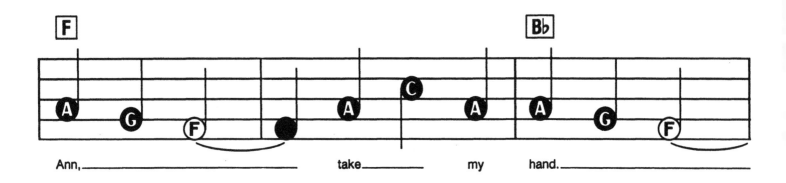

Ann,_____ take_____ my hand._____

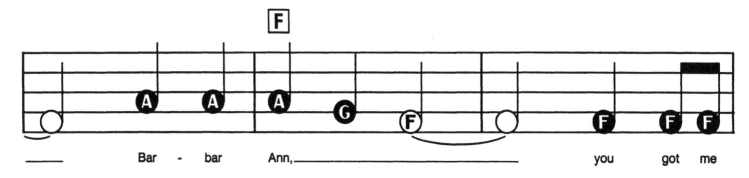

_____ Bar - bar Ann,_____ you got me

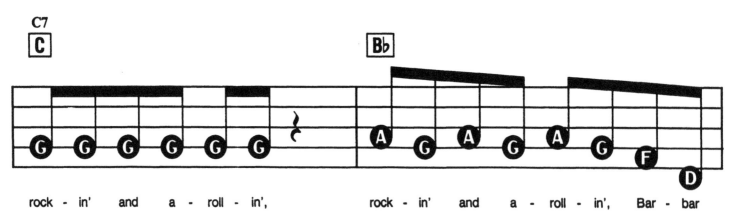

rock - in' and a - roll - in',   rock - in' and a - roll - in', Bar - bar

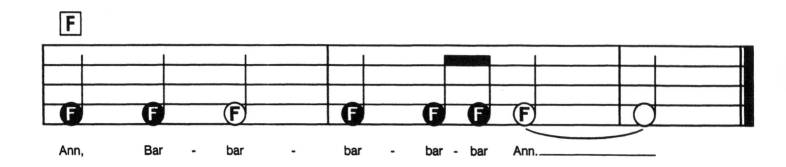

Ann,   Bar - bar - bar - bar-bar Ann._____

California Girls

Registration 7
Rhythm: Rock

Words and Music by Brian Wilson
and Mike Love

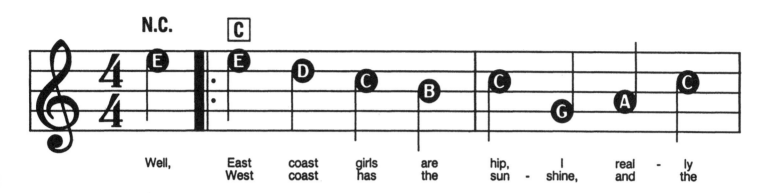

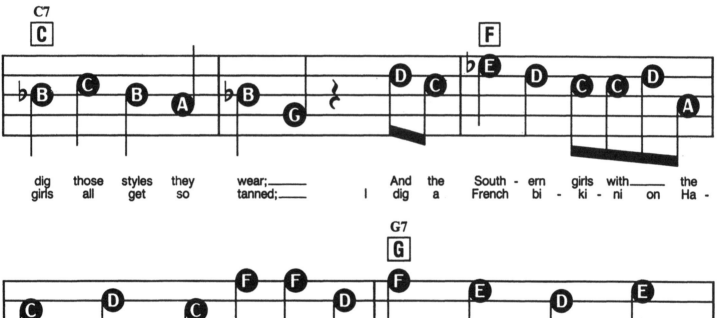

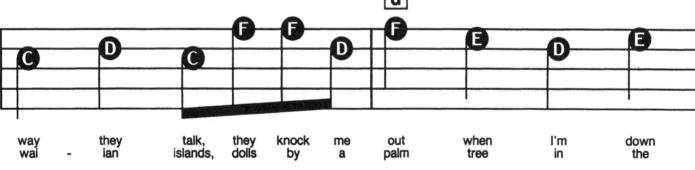

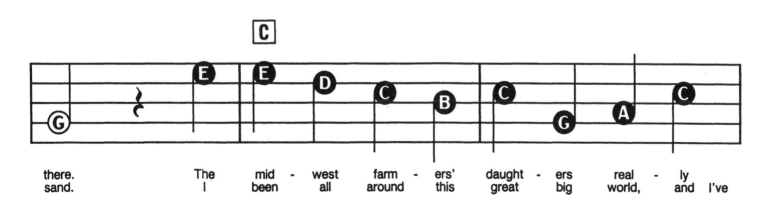

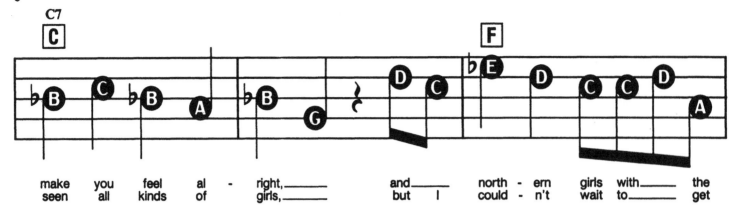

make you feel al - right,_____ and_____ north - ern girls with_____ the
seen all kinds of girls,_____ but I could - n't wait to_____ get

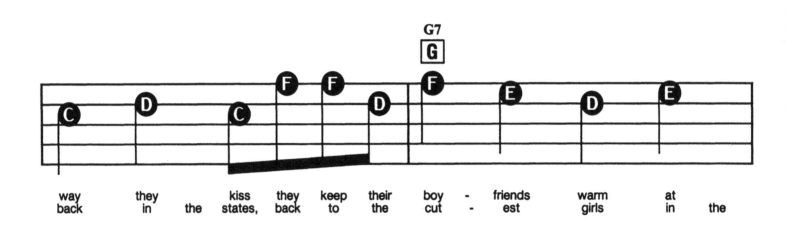

way they kiss they keep their boy - friends warm at
back in the states, they back to the cut - est girls in the

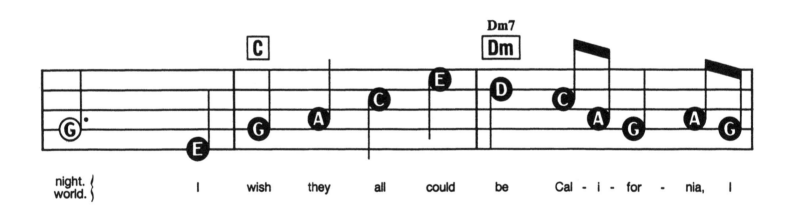

night. I wish they all could be Cal - i - for - nia, I
world.

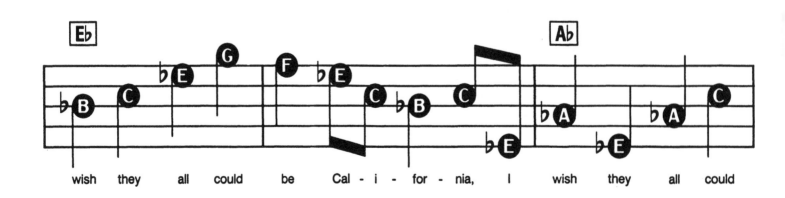

wish they all could be Cal - i - for - nia, I wish they all could

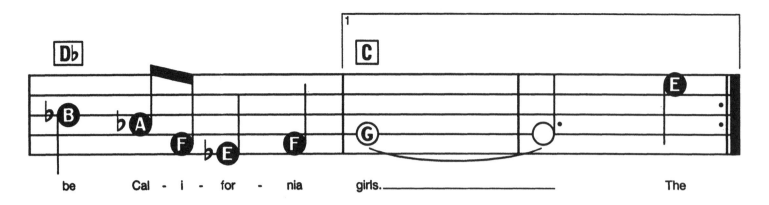

be Cal - i - for - nia girls._____ The

girls._____ I

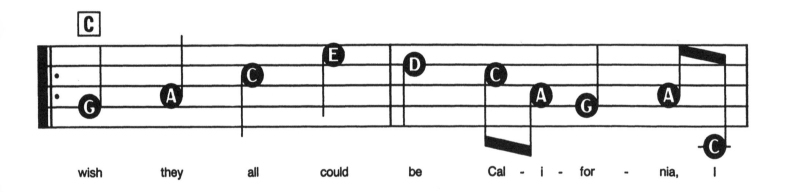

wish they all could be Cal - i - for - nia, I

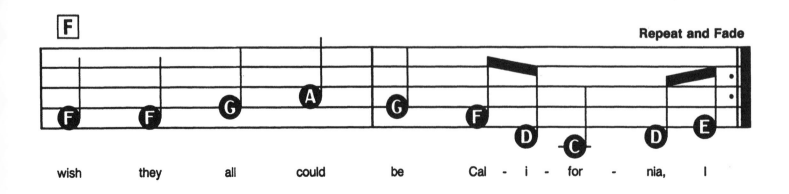

Repeat and Fade

wish they all could be Cal - i - for - nia, I

Dance, Dance, Dance

Registration 7
Rhythm: Rock

Words and Music by Brian Wilson,
Carl Wilson and Mike Love

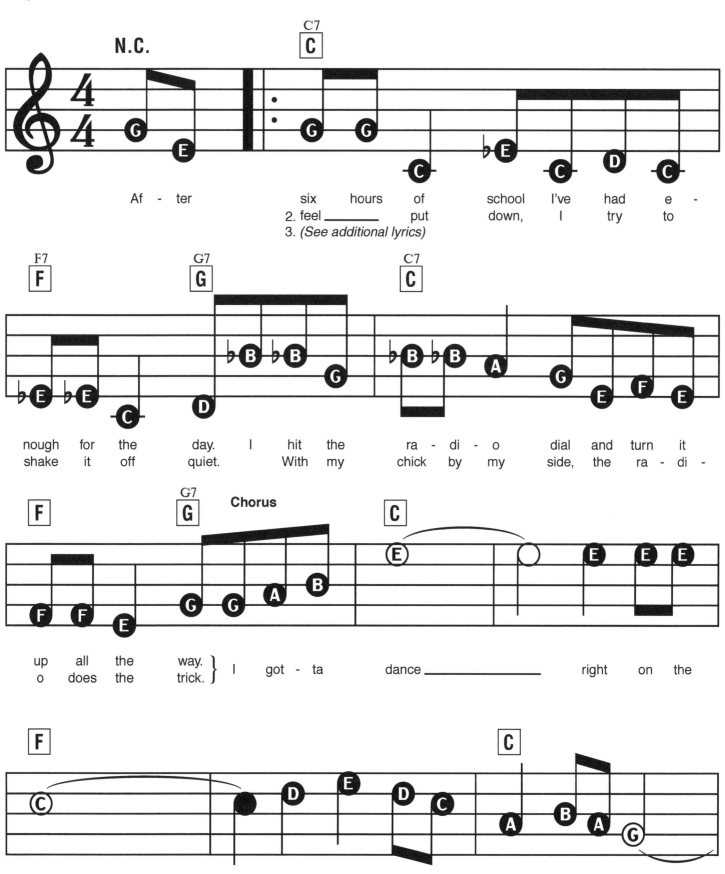

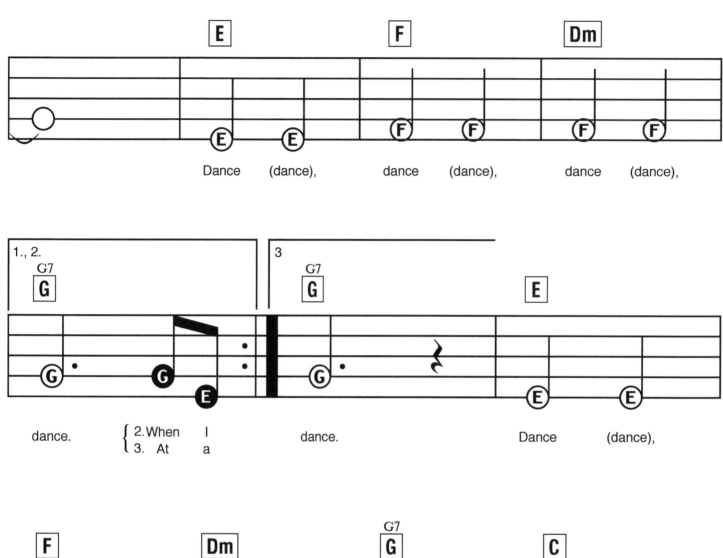

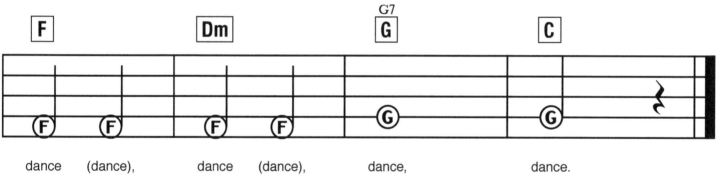

Additional Lyrics

3. At a weekend dance, we like to show up last.
I play it cool when it's slow and jump it when it's fast.
Chorus

Do It Again

Registration 7
Rhythm: Rock

Words and Music by Brian Wilson
and Mike Love

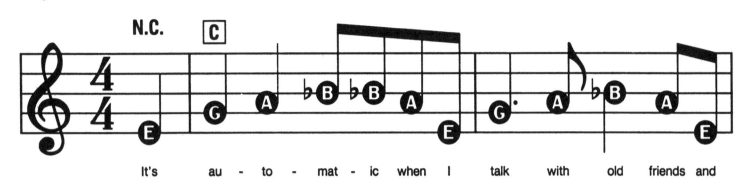

It's au - to - mat - ic when I talk with old friends and

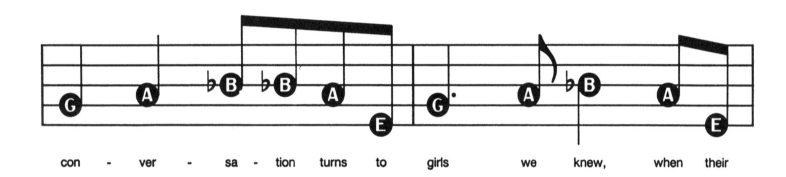

con - ver - sa - tion turns to girls we knew, when their

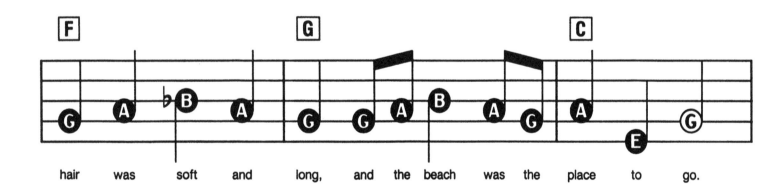

hair was soft and long, and the beach was the place to go.

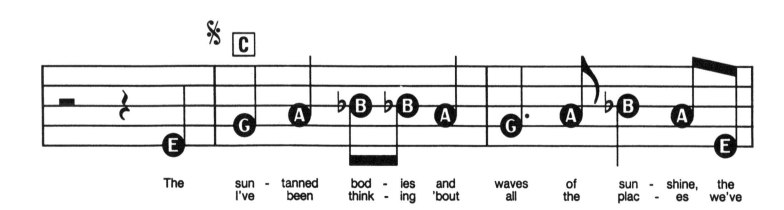

The sun - tanned bod - ies and waves of sun - shine, the
I've been think - ing 'bout all the plac - es we've

13

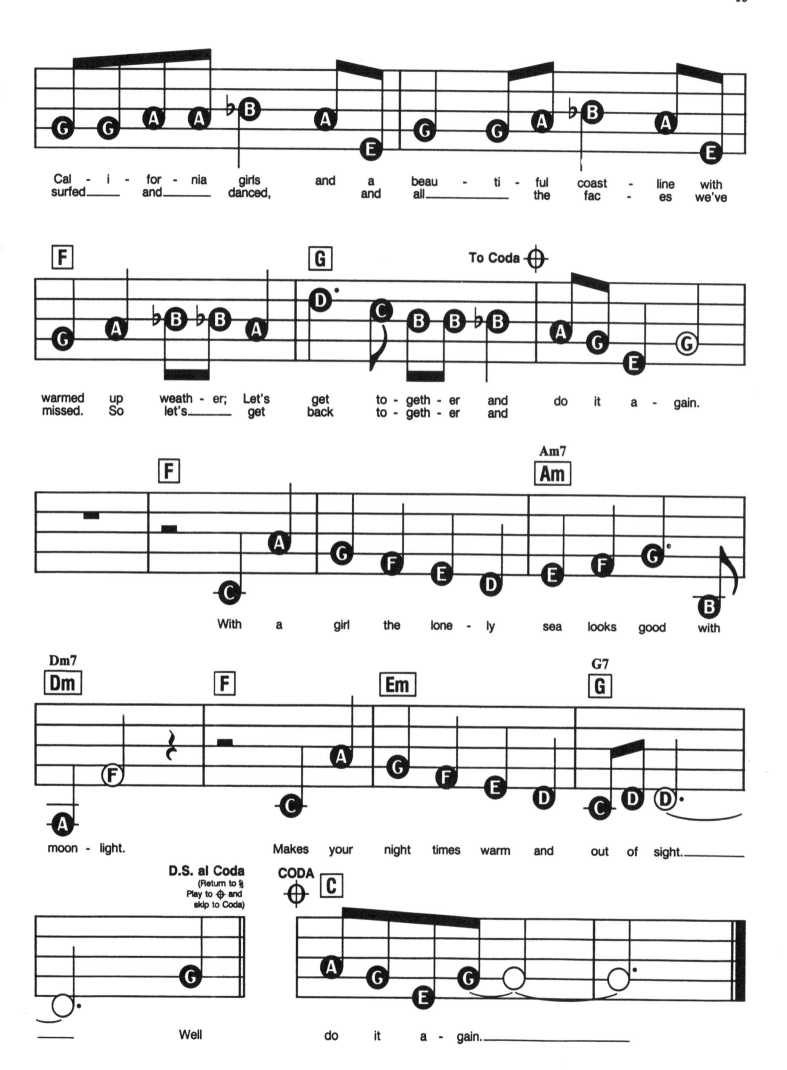

Don't Back Down

Registration 7
Rhythm: Rock

Words and Music by Brian Wilson
and Mike Love

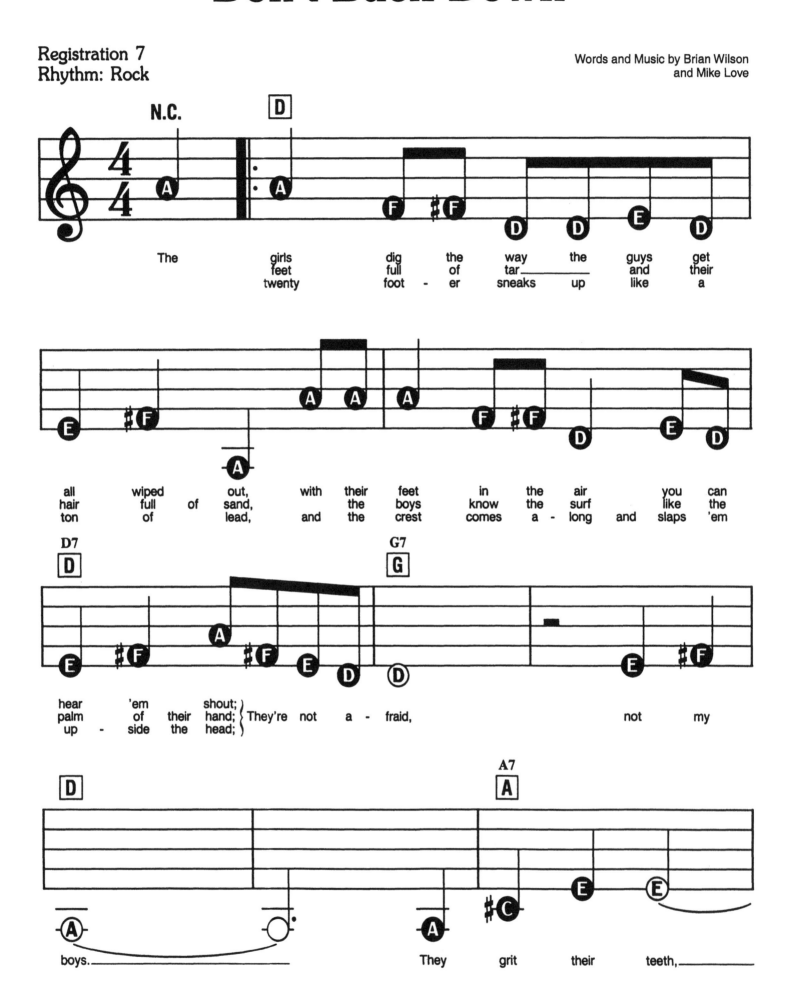

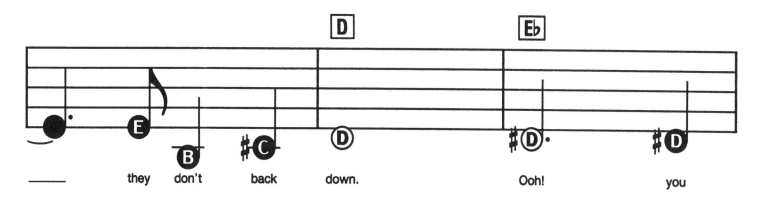

they don't back down. Ooh! you

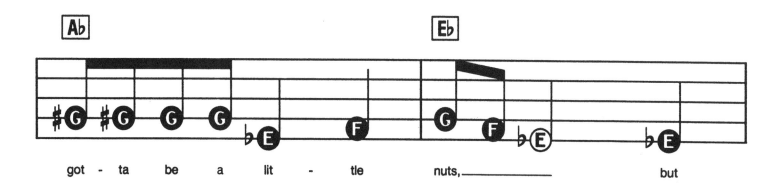

got - ta be a lit - tle nuts,_____ but

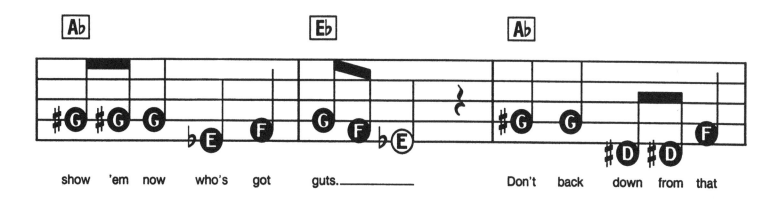

show 'em now who's got guts._____ Don't back down from that

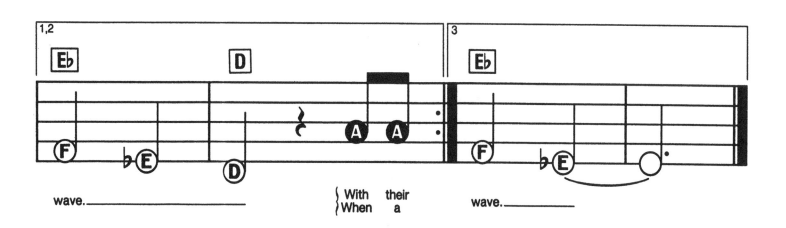

wave._____ With their / When a wave._____

Don't Worry Baby

Registration 7
Rhythm: Rock

Words and Music by Brian Wilson, Roger Christian, Mitchell Margo, Philip Margo, Henry Medress and Jay Siegel

Well, it's been build - in' up in - side of me for
should - a kept my mouth shut when I
ba - by, when you race to - day, just

oh, I don't know how long.
start to brag a - bout my car.
take a - long my love with you.

But I don't know
And if you can't

why, but I keep think - in' some - thing's bound to go wrong.
back down now be - cause I pushed the oth - er guys too far.
knew how much I loved you, ba - by, noth - ing could go wrong with you."

But she looks in my eyes and makes me
She makes me come a - live and makes me
Oh what she does to me when she makes

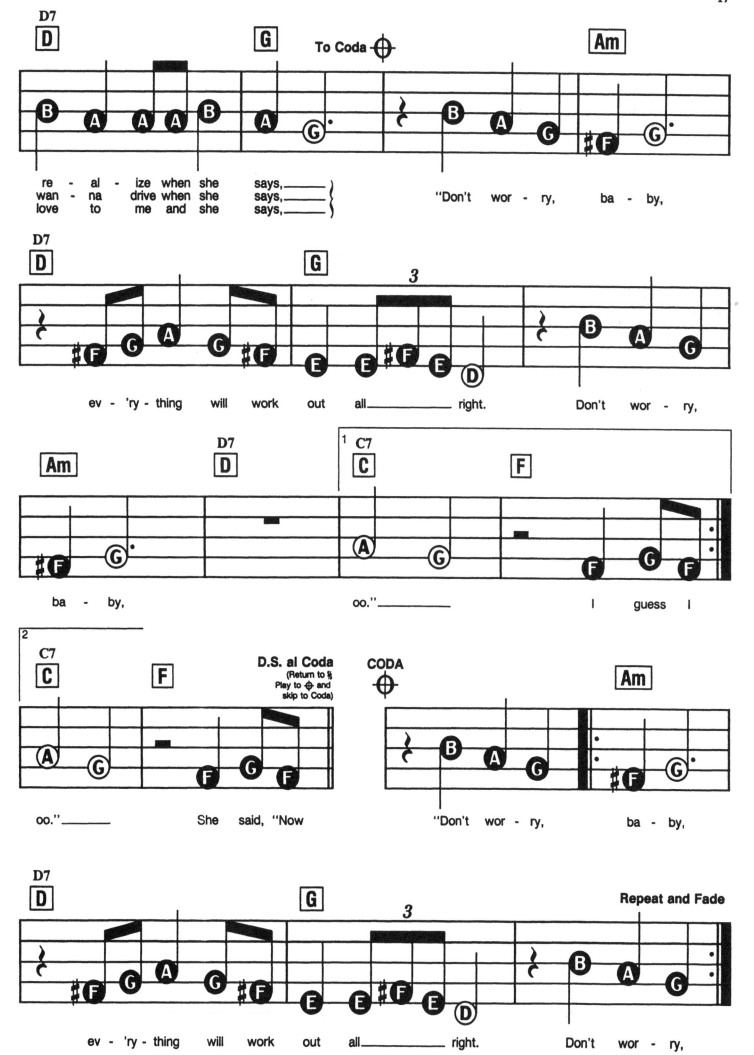

Fun, Fun, Fun

Registration 7
Rhythm: Rock

Words and Music by Brian Wilson
and Mike Love

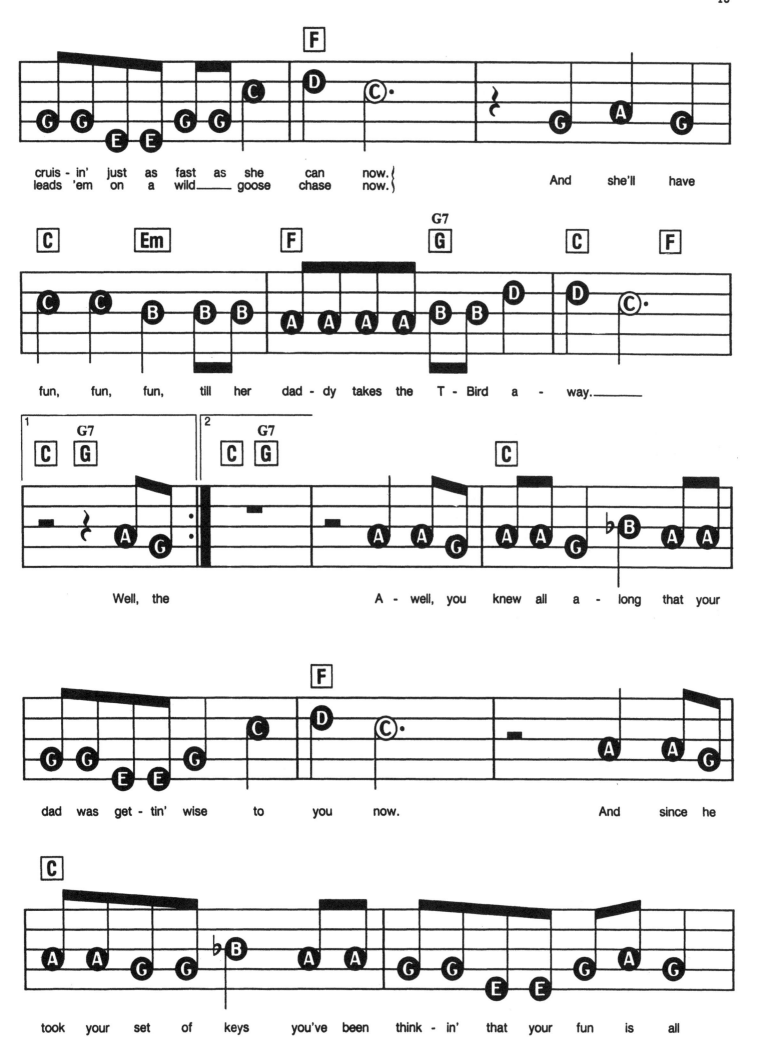

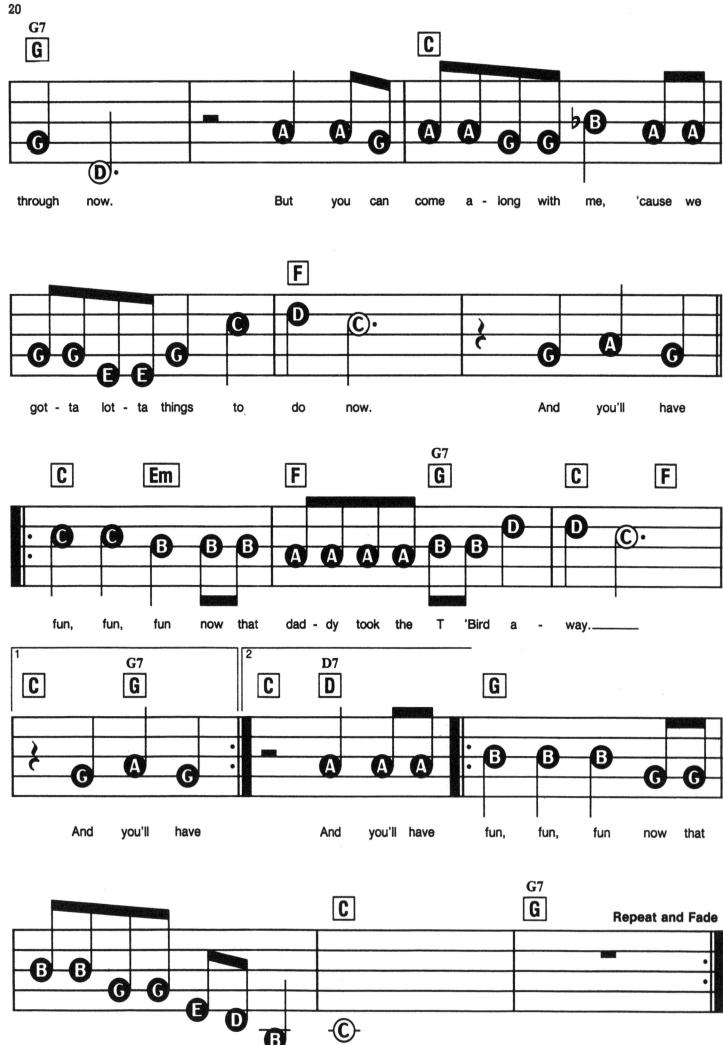

Good Vibrations

Registration 7
Rhythm: Rock

Words and Music by Brian Wilson
and Mike Love

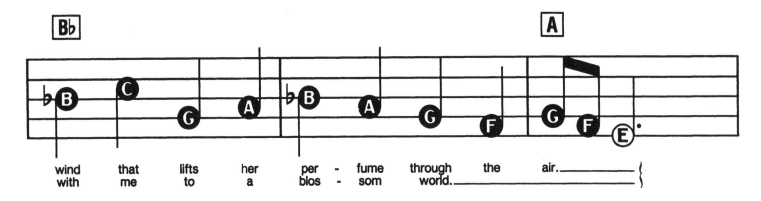

wind that lifts her per - fume through the air._____
with me to a blos - som world._____

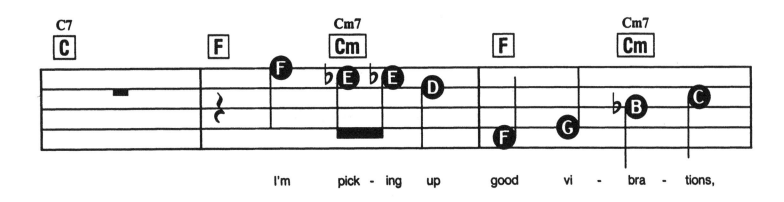

I'm pick - ing up good vi - bra - tions,

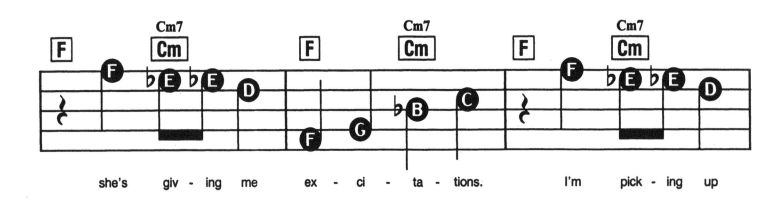

she's giv - ing me ex - ci - ta - tions. I'm pick - ing up

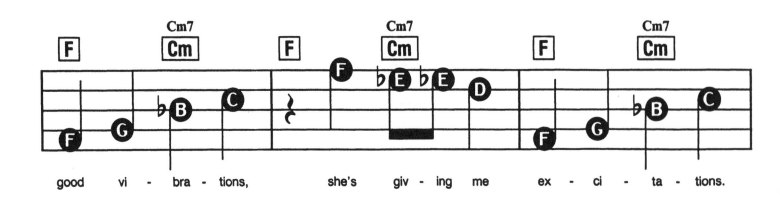

good vi - bra - tions, she's giv - ing me ex - ci - ta - tions.

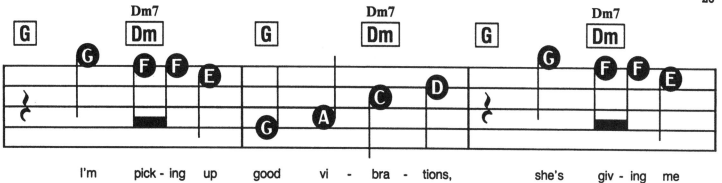

I'm pick - ing up good vi - bra - tions, she's giv - ing me

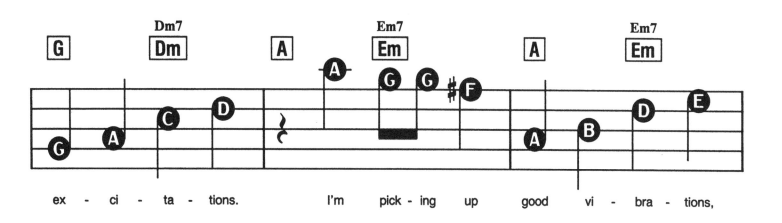

ex - ci - ta - tions. I'm pick - ing up good vi - bra - tions,

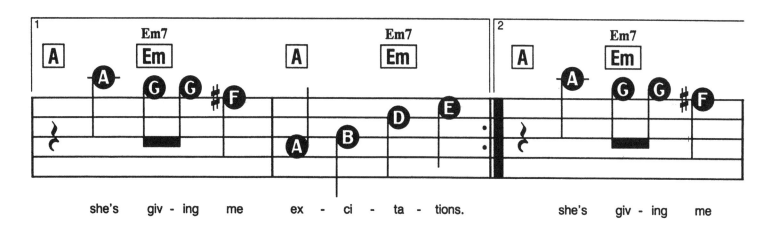

she's giv - ing me ex - ci - ta - tions. she's giv - ing me

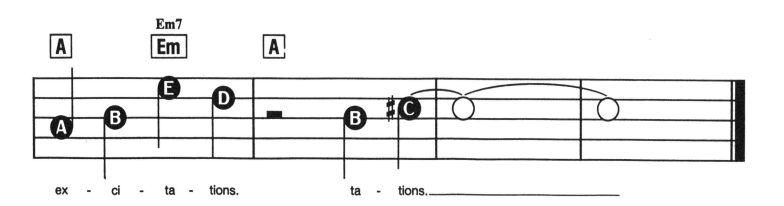

ex - ci - ta - tions. ta - tions.

Help Me Rhonda

Registration 7
Rhythm: Rock

Words and Music by Brian Wilson
and Mike Love

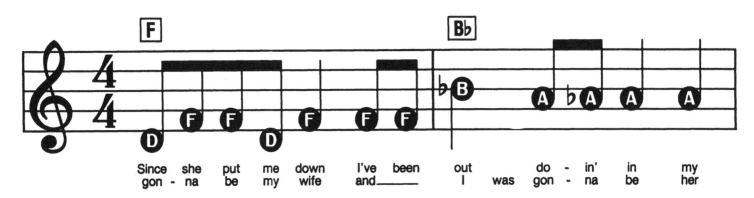

Since she put me down I've been out

do - in' in my

gon - na be my wife and_____ I was gon - na be her

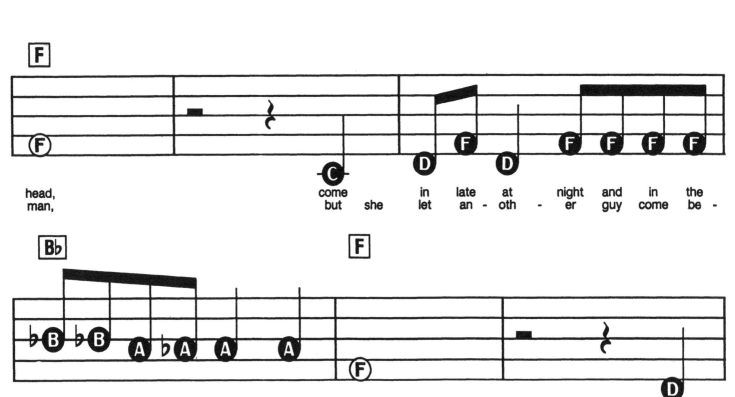

head,

come in late at night and in the

man,

but she let an - oth - er guy come be -

morn - in' I just lay in bed.

Well,

tween us and it ruined our plans.

Well,

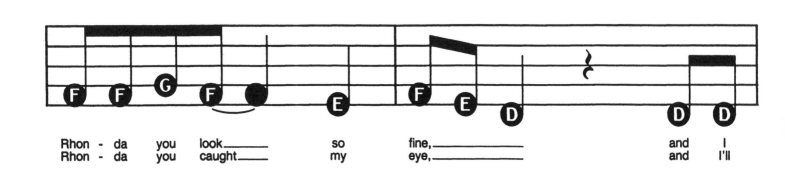

Rhon - da you look_____ so fine,_____ and I

Rhon - da you caught_____ my eye,_____ and I'll

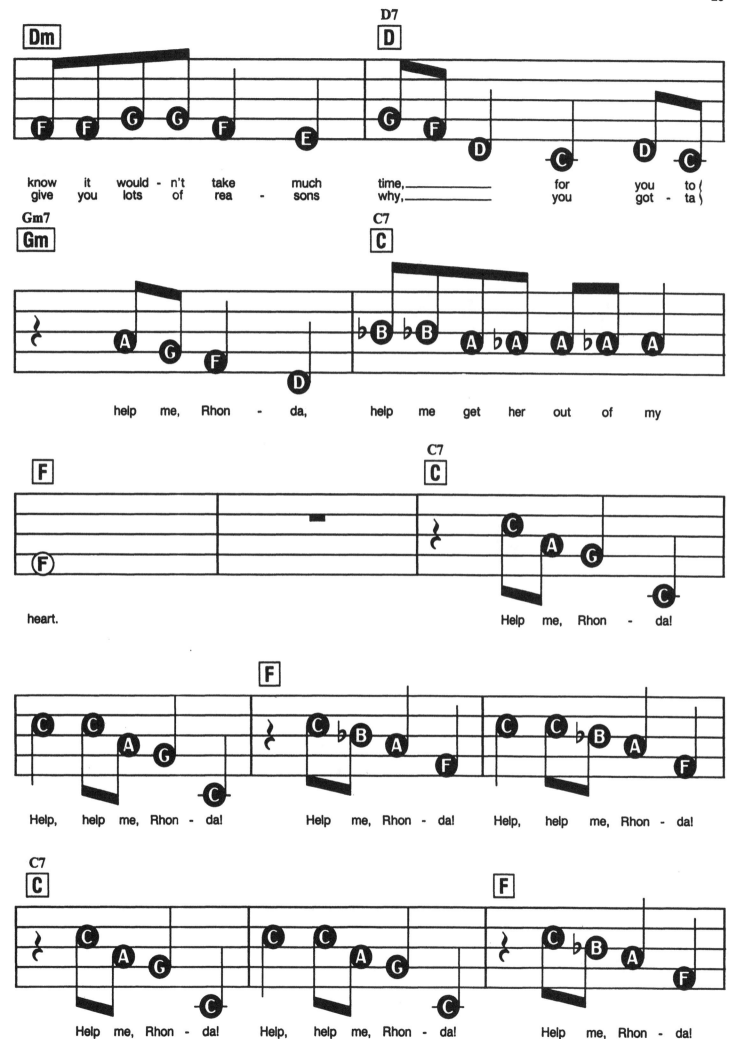

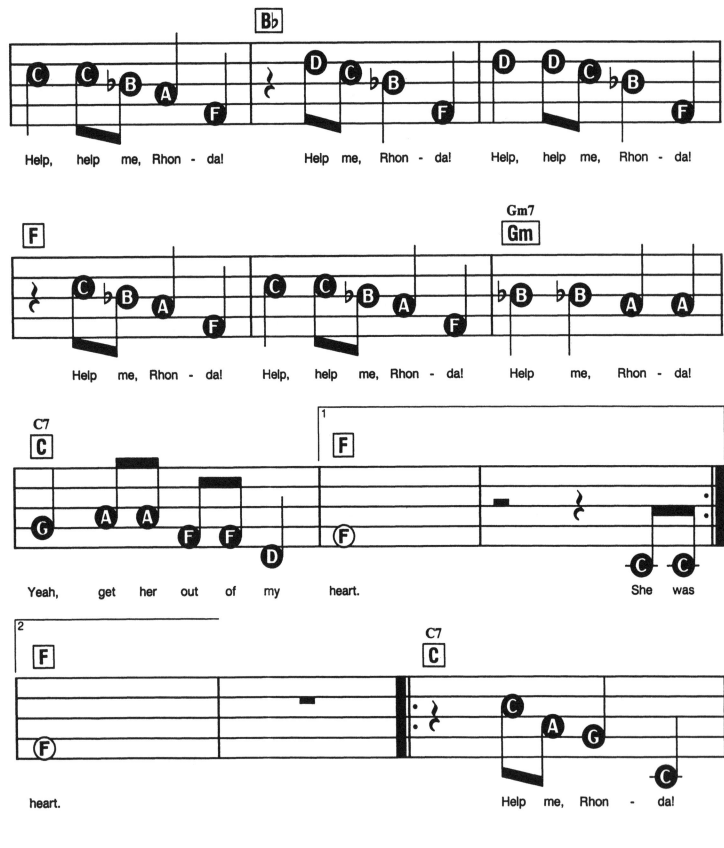

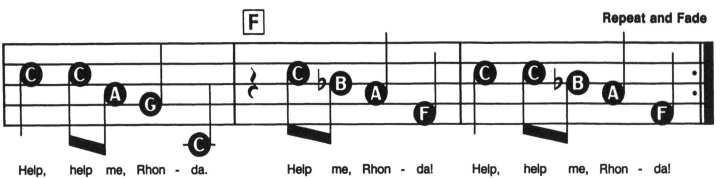

Kokomo
from the Motion Picture COCKTAIL

Registration 7
Rhythm: Bossa Nova or Latin

Words and Music by Mike Love, Terry Melcher,
John Phillips and Scott McKenzie

A - ru - ba, Ja - mai - ca, Oo_____ I wan - na take ya. Ber -

mu - da, Ba - ha - ma, come_____ on, pret - ty ma - ma. Key

Lar - go, Mon - te - go, Ba - by, why don't we go, Ja -

mai - ca. Off the Flor - i - da Keys_____

There's a place called Ko - ko - mo. That's where you

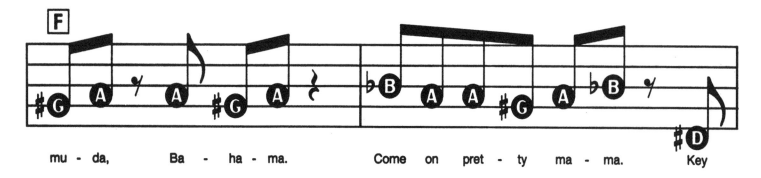

mu - da, Ba - ha - ma. Come on pret - ty ma - ma. Key

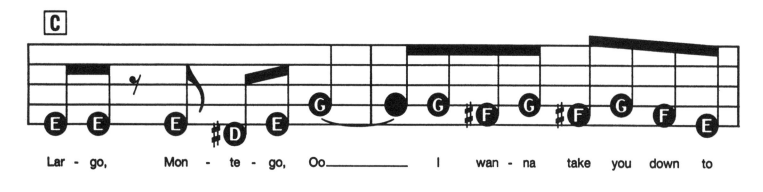

Lar - go, Mon - te - go, Oo_____ I wan - na take you down to

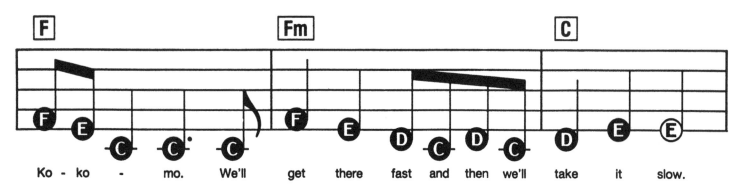

Ko - ko - mo. We'll get there fast and then we'll take it slow.

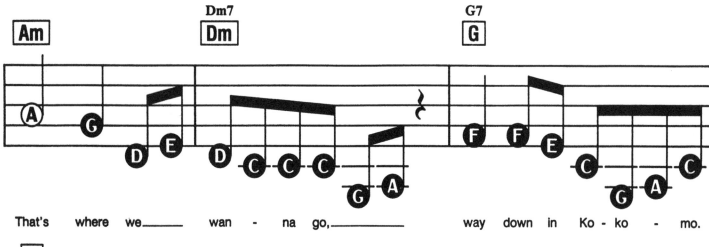

That's where we_____ wan - na go,_____ way down in Ko - ko - mo.

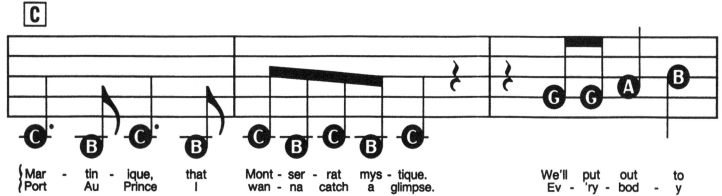

Mar - tin - ique, that Mont - ser - rat mys - tique.
Port Au Prince I wan - na catch a glimpse.
We'll put out to
Ev - 'ry - bod - y

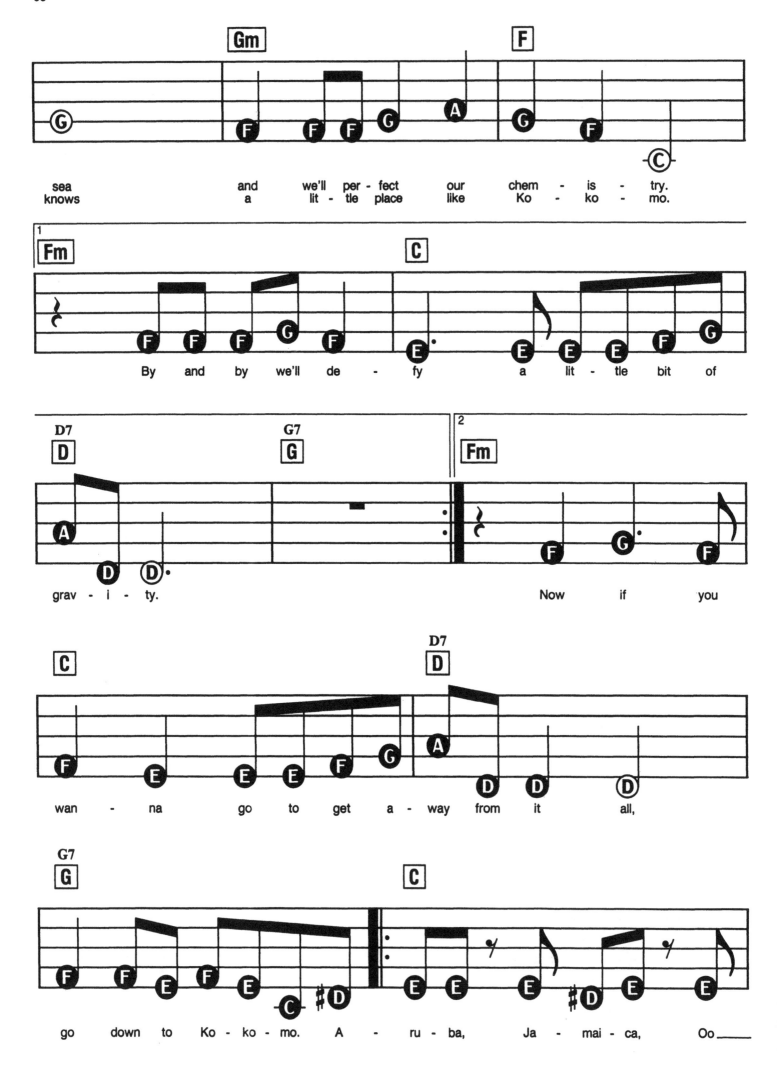

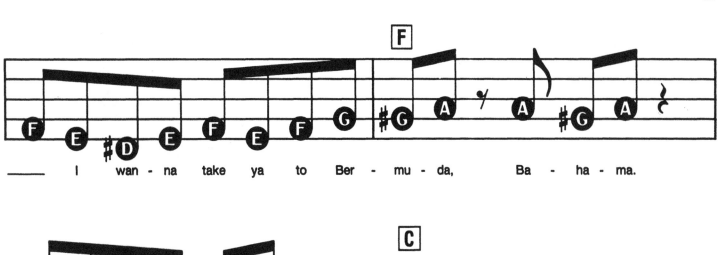

_____ I wan - na take ya to Ber - mu - da, Ba - ha - ma.

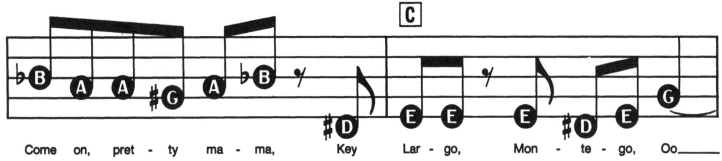

Come on, pret - ty ma - ma, Key Lar - go, Mon - te - go, Oo_____

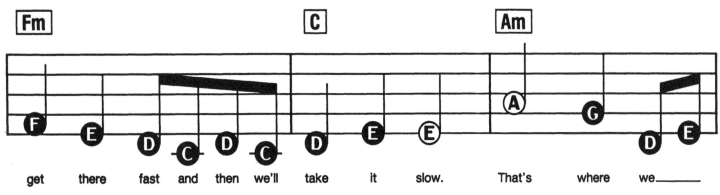

_____ I wan - na take you down to Ko - ko - mo. We'll

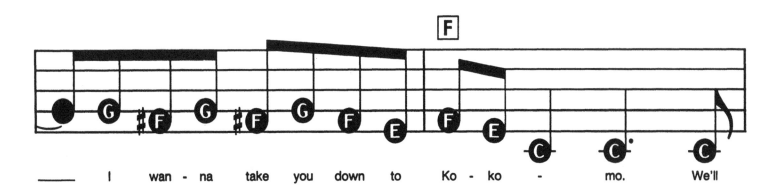

get there fast and then we'll take it slow. That's where we_____

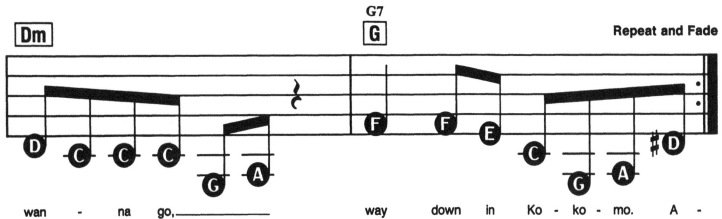

wan - na go,_____ way down in Ko - ko - mo. A -

I Get Around

Registration 7
Rhythm: Rock

Words and Music by Brian Wilson
and Mike Love

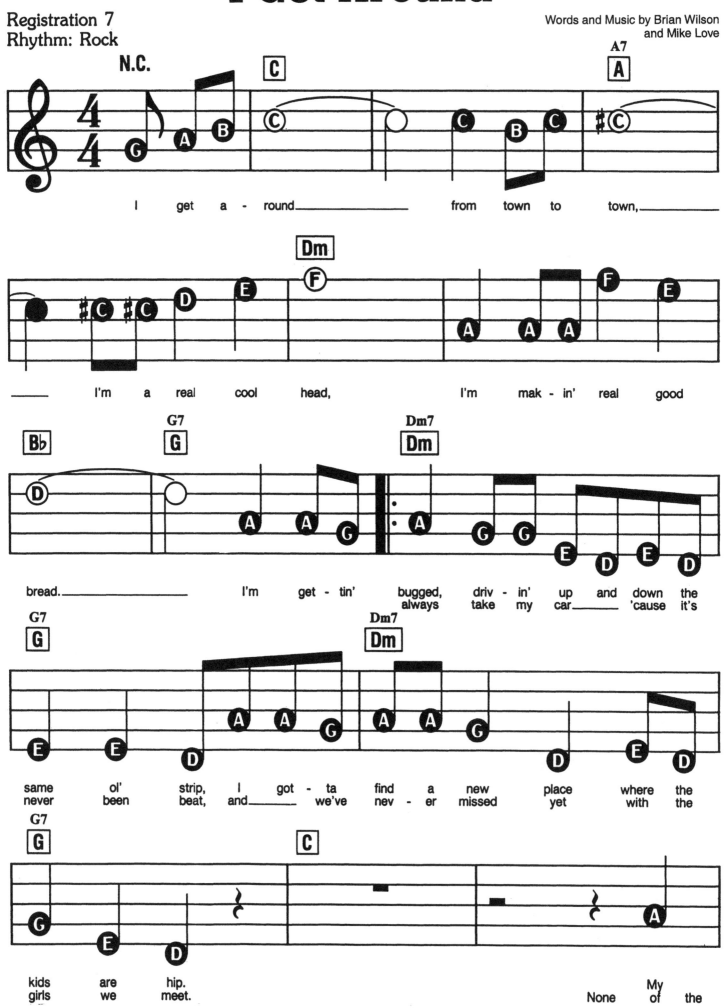

bud - dies and me are get - tin' real well - known, yeah, the
guys_____ go stead - y 'cause it wouldn't be right, to leave your

bad guys know us and they leave us a - lone.⎫
best girl home_____ on a Sat - ur - day night.⎭ I get a - round_____

_____ from town to town,_____ I'm a real cool

head, I'm mak - in' real good bread._____

We _____

(Spoken:) I get around, etc.

In My Room

Registration 1
Rhythm: Slow Rock or Ballad

Words and Music by Brian Wilson
and Gary Usher

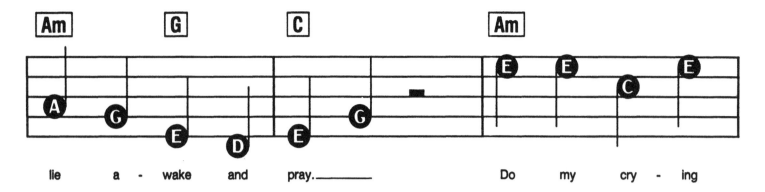

lie a - wake and pray._____ Do my cry - ing

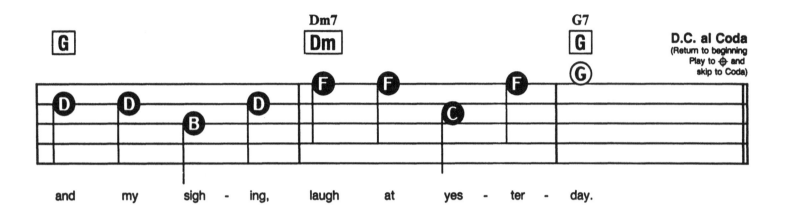

and my sigh - ing, laugh at yes - ter - day.

D.C. al Coda
(Return to beginning
Play to ⊕ and
skip to Coda)

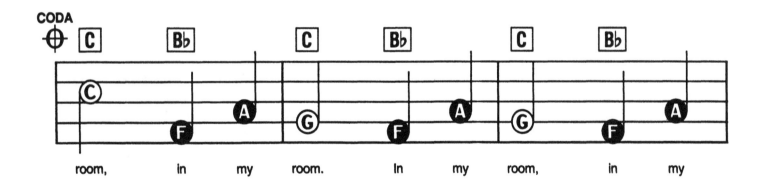

room, in my room. In my room, in my

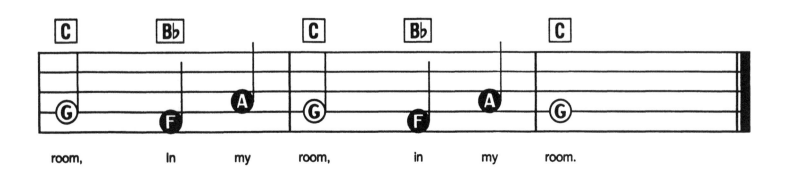

room, In my room, in my room.

Little Deuce Coupe

Registration 4
Rhythm: Rock

Music by Brian Wilson
Words by Roger Christian

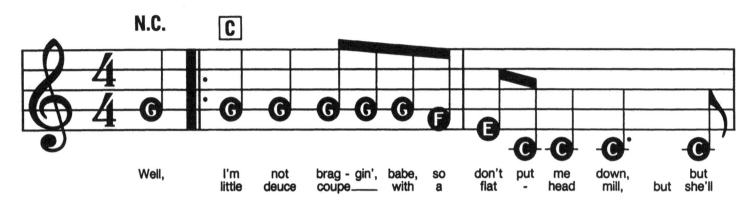

Well,   I'm not brag - gin', babe, so   don't put me down,   but
little   deuce coupe___ with a   flat - head mill,   but she'll

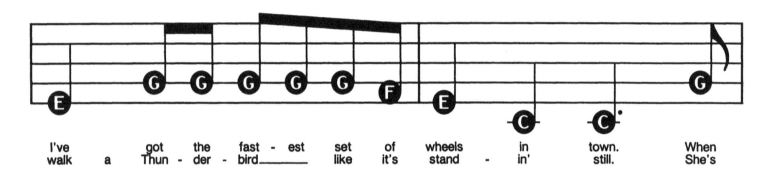

I've   got the fast - est set of wheels   in   town.   When
walk a Thun - der - bird___ like it's stand - in' still.   She's

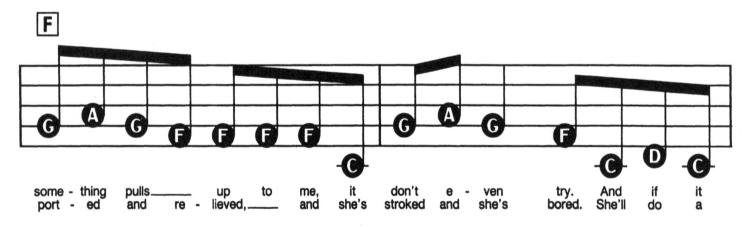

some - thing pulls___ up to me, it don't e - ven   try. And if it
port - ed and re - lieved,___ and she's stroked and she's bored. She'll do a

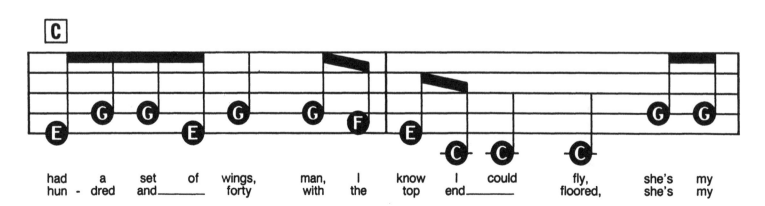

had a set of wings, man, I know I could   fly, she's my
hun - dred and___ forty with the top end___ floored, she's my

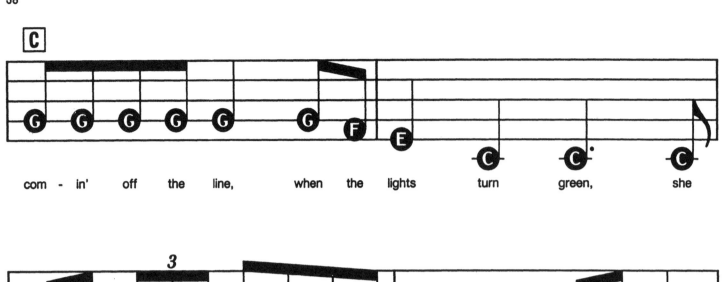

com - in' off the line, when the lights turn green, she

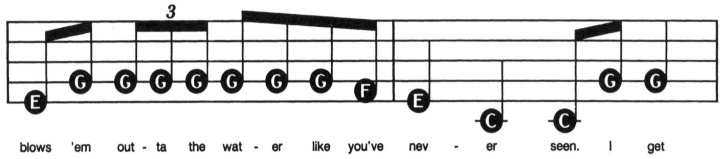

blows 'em out - ta the wat - er like you've nev - er seen. I get

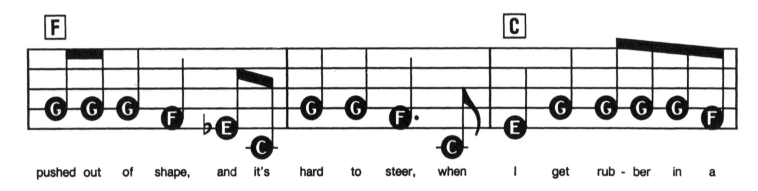

pushed out of shape, and it's hard to steer, when I get rub - ber in a

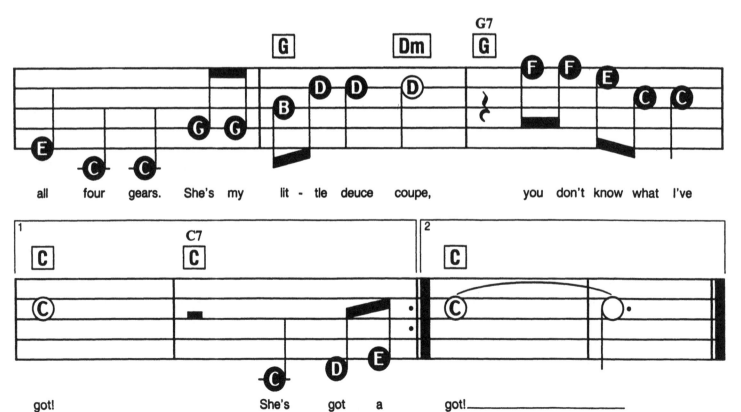

all four gears. She's my lit - tle deuce coupe, you don't know what I've

got! She's got a got!_____

Shut Down

Registration 4
Rhythm: Rock

Words by Roger Christian
Music by Brian Wilson

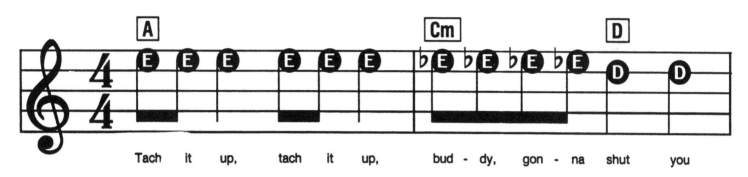

Tach it up, tach it up, bud - dy, gon - na shut you

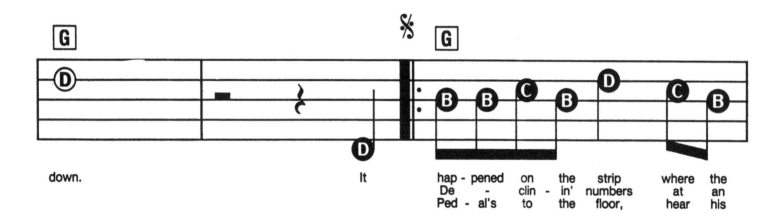

down. It
hap - pened on the strip, where the
De - clin - in' numbers at an
Ped - al's to the floor, hear his

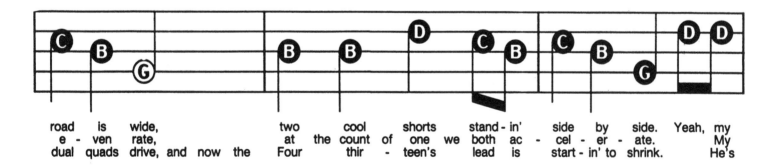

road is wide, two cool shorts stand - in' side by side. Yeah, my
e - ven rate, at the count of one we both ac - cel - er - ate. My
dual quads drive, and now the Four thir - teen's lead is start - in' to shrink. He's

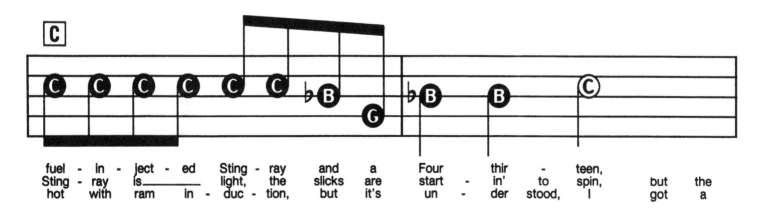

fuel - in - ject - ed Sting - ray and a
Sting - ray is light, the slicks are
hot with ram in - duc - tion, but it's

Four thir - teen,
start - in' to spin, but the
un - der stood, I got a

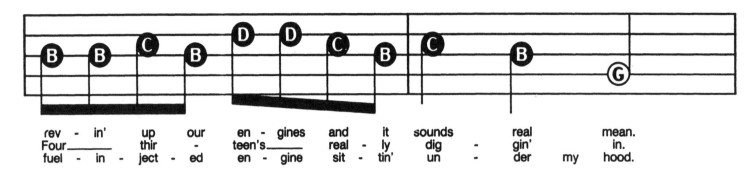

rev - in' up our en - gines and it sounds real mean.
Four____ thir - teen's____ real - ly dig - gin' in.
fuel - in - ject - ed en - gine sit - tin' un - der my hood.

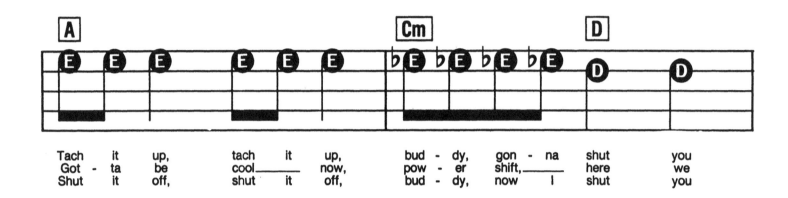

Tach it up, tach it up, bud - dy, gon - na shut you
Got - ta be cool____ now, pow - er shift,____ here we
Shut it off, shut it off, bud - dy, now I shut you

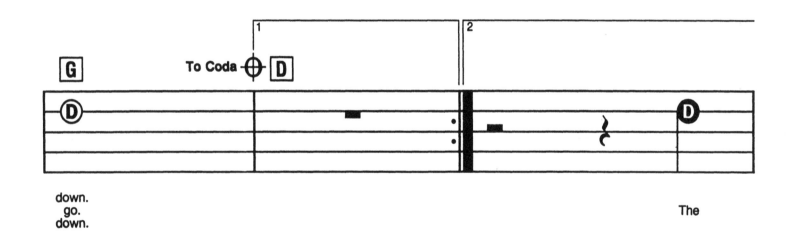

down.
go.
down.

The

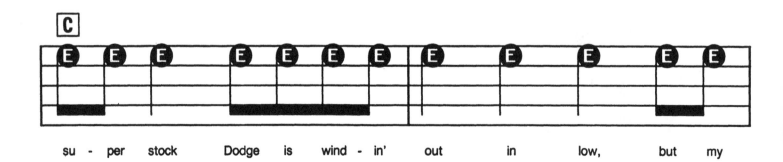

su - per stock Dodge is wind - in' out in low, but my

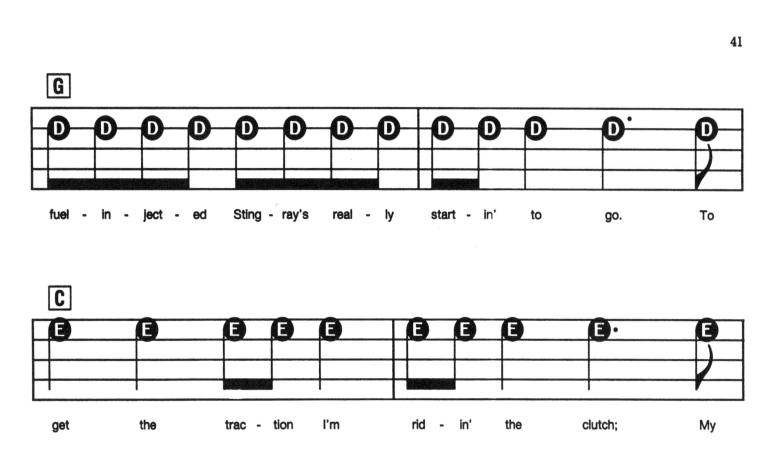

fuel - in - ject - ed Sting - ray's real - ly start - in' to go. To

get the trac - tion I'm rid - in' the clutch; My

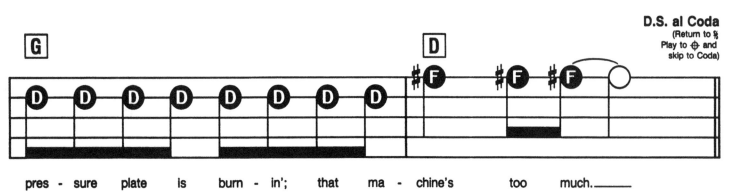

D.S. al Coda
(Return to %
Play to ⊕ and
skip to Coda)

pres - sure plate is burn - in'; that ma - chine's too much.____

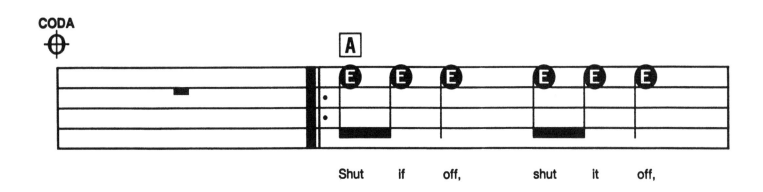

Shut if off, shut it off,

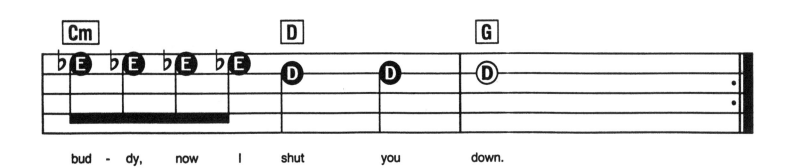

bud - dy, now I shut you down.

Sloop John B

Registration 2
Rhythm: Calypso or Reggae

Words and Music by
Brian Wilson

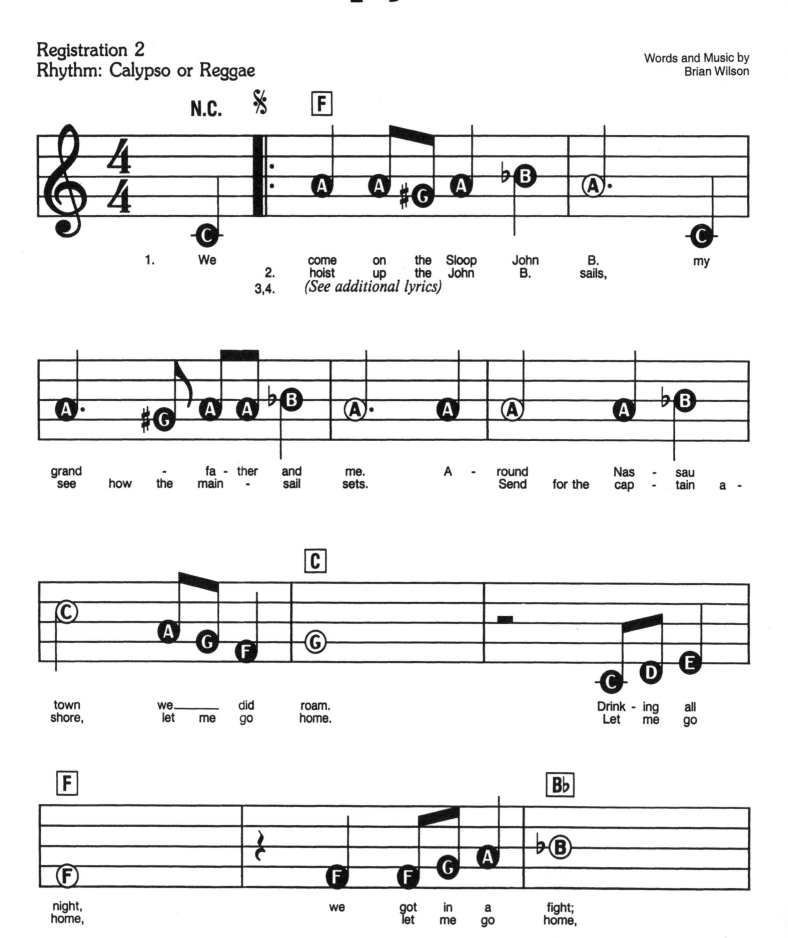

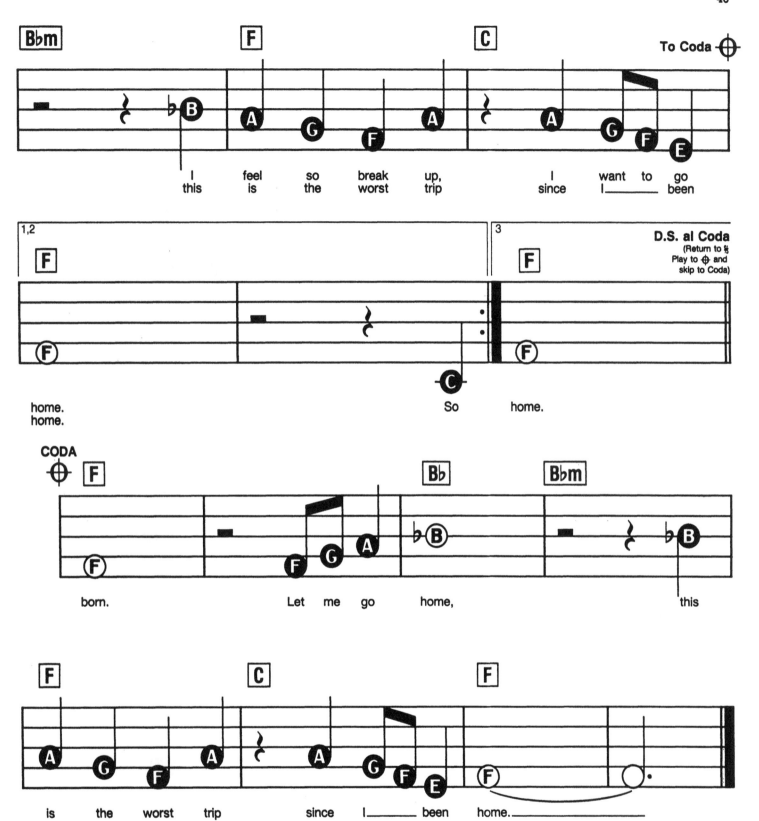

Additional Lyrics

3. The first mate, he got drunk,
Broke in the Captain's trunk.
Constable had to come and take him away,
Sheriff John Stone, please let me alone,
I feel so break up, I want to go home.

4. The poor cook, he took fits,
Throw away all the grits.
Then he took and ate up all of the corn,
Sheriff John Stone, please let me alone,
This is the worst trip since I been born.

Surfer Girl

Registration 1
Rhythm: Slow Rock or Rock 'N' Roll

Words and Music by
Brian Wilson

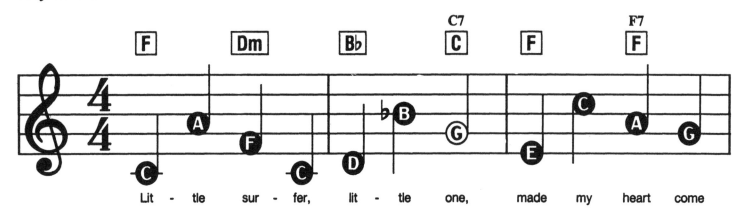

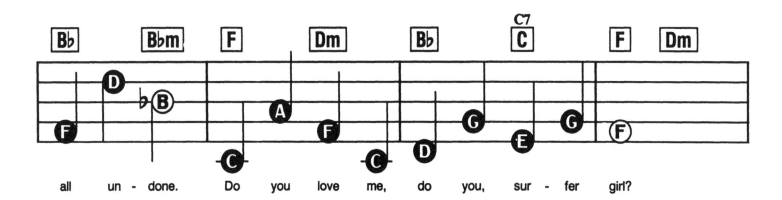

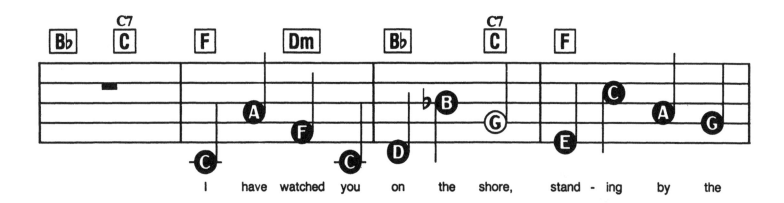

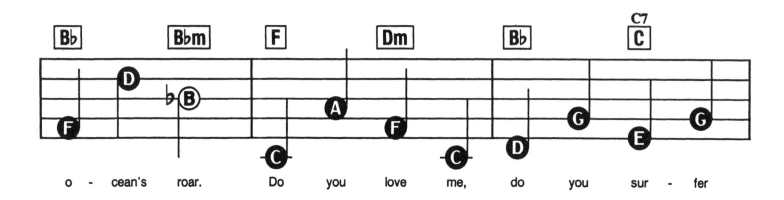

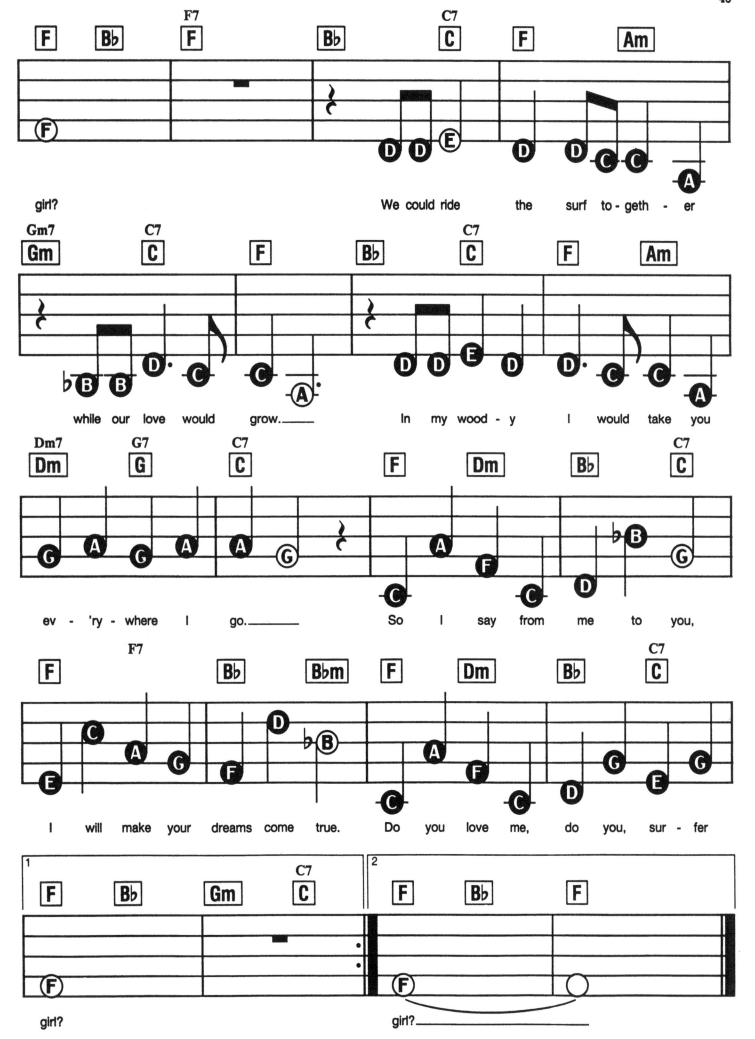

girl?

We could ride   the   surf to - geth - er

while   our   love   would   grow._____   In   my   wood - y   I   would   take   you

ev - 'ry - where   I   go. _____   So   I   say   from   me   to   you,

I   will   make   your   dreams   come   true.   Do   you   love   me,   do   you,   sur - fer

girl?   girl?_____

Surfin' U.S.A.

Registration 4
Rhythm: Rock or Fox Trot

Words and Music by
Chuck Berry

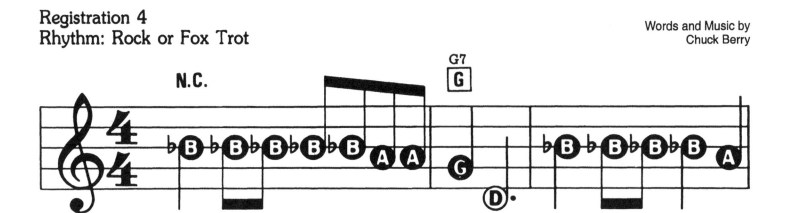

If ev - 'ry - bod - y had an o - cean a - cross the U. S.

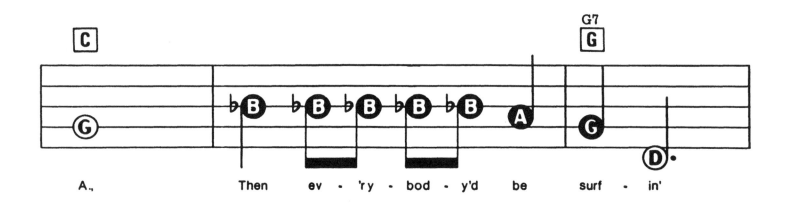

A., Then ev - 'ry - bod - y'd be surf - in'

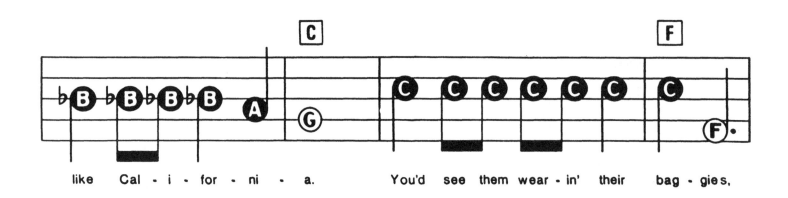

like Cal - i - for - ni - a. You'd see them wear - in' their bag - gies,

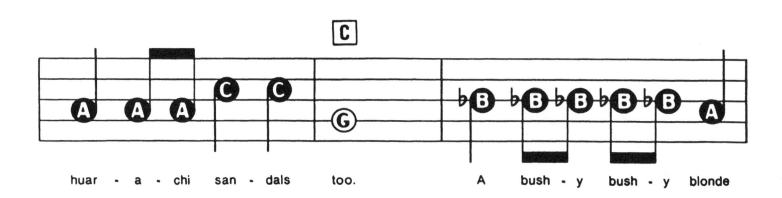

huar - a - chi san - dals too. A bush - y bush - y blonde

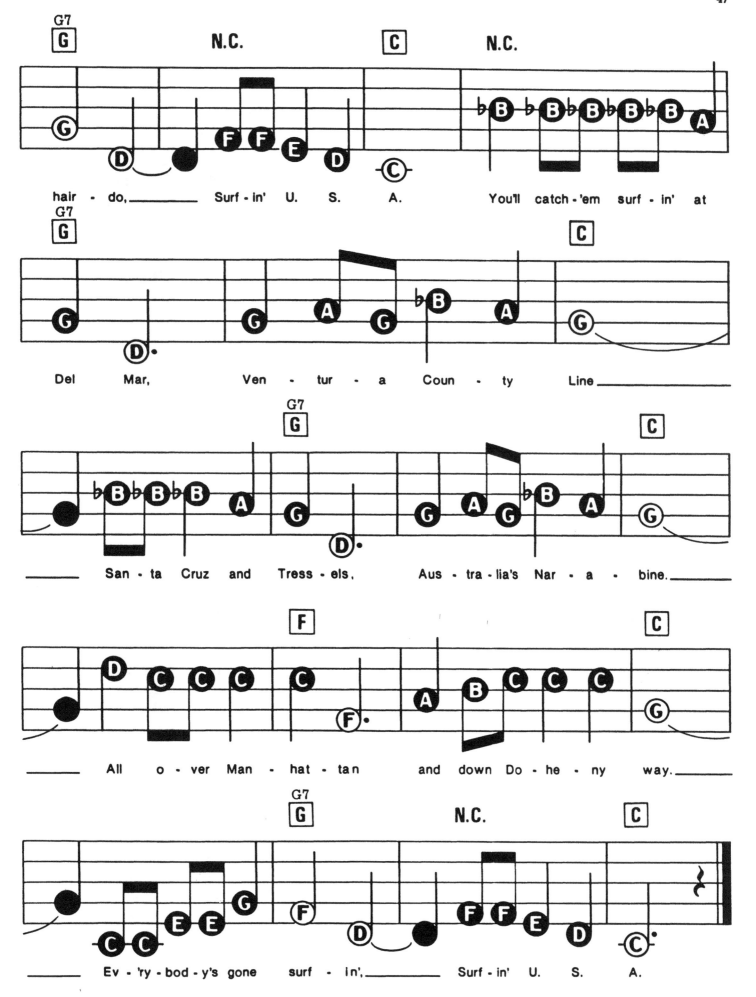

Surfin' Safari

Registration 4
Rhythm: Rock or Swing

Words and Music by Brian Wilson
and Mike Love

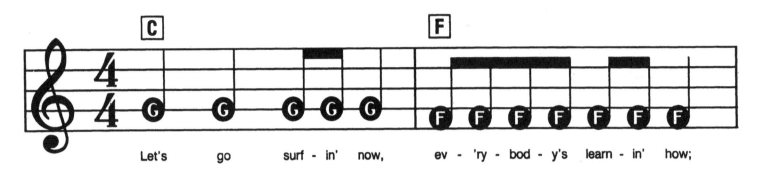

Let's go surf - in' now, ev - 'ry - bod - y's learn - in' how;

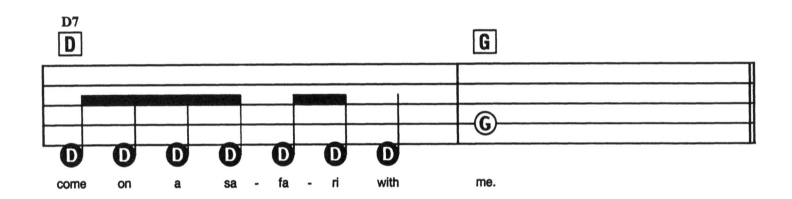

come on a sa - fa - ri with me.

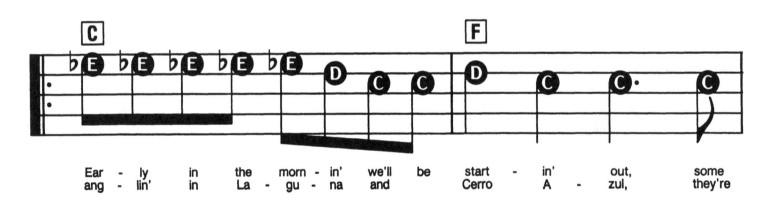

Ear - ly in the morn - in' we'll be start - in' out, some
ang - lin' in La - gu - na and Cerro A - zul, they're

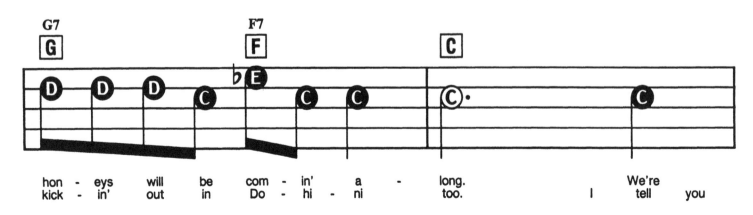

hon - eys will be com - in' a - long. We're
kick - in' out in Do - hi - ni too. I tell you

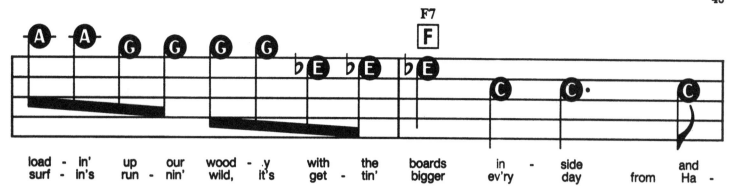

load - in' up our wood - .y with the boards in - side and
surf - in's run - nin' wild, it's get - tin' bigger ev'ry day from Ha -

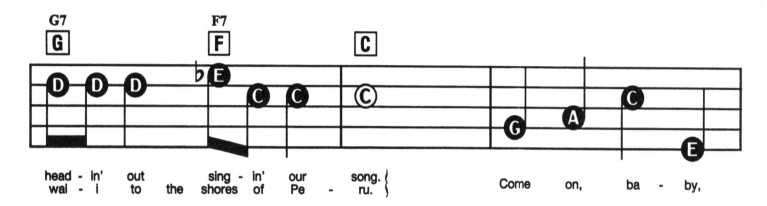

head - in' out sing - in' our song. Come on, ba - by,
wai - i to the shores of Pe - ru.

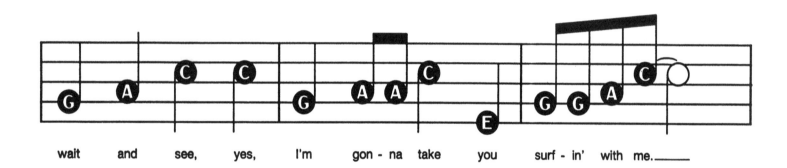

wait and see, yes, I'm gon - na take you surf - in' with me.____

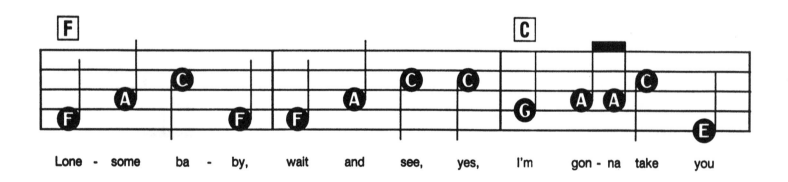

Lone - some ba - by, wait and see, yes, I'm gon - na take you

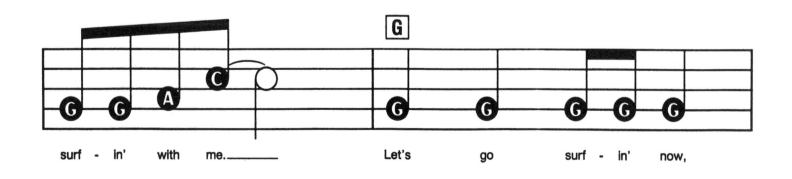

surf - in' with me.____ Let's go surf - in' now,

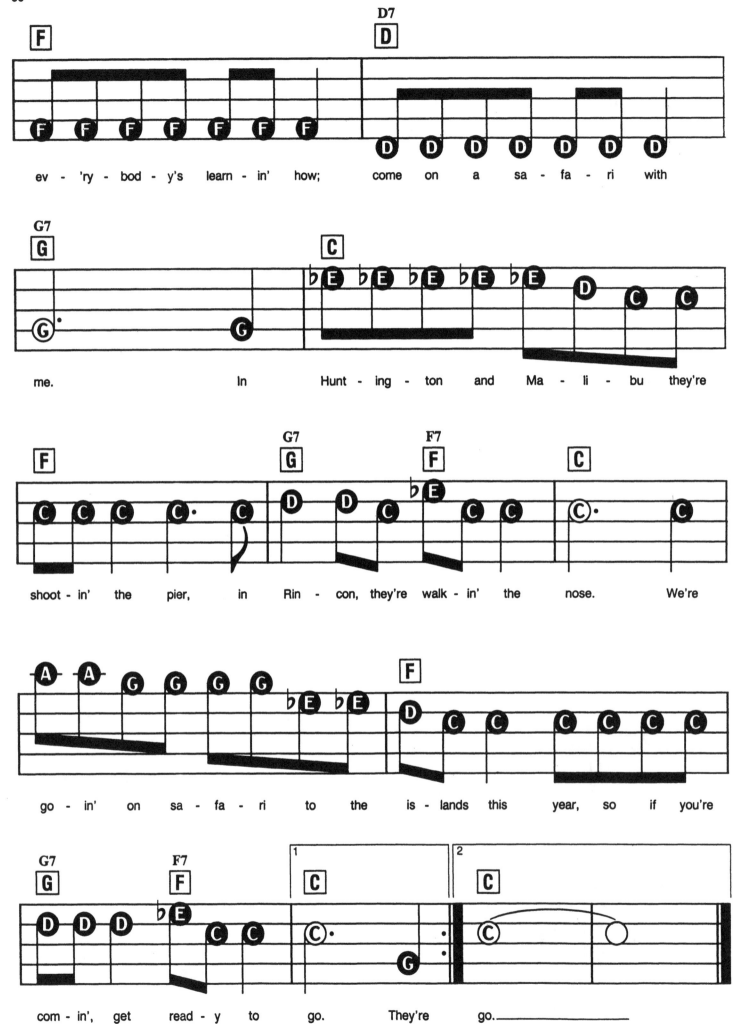

When I Grow Up
(To Be a Man)

Registration 7
Rhythm: Rock

Words and Music by Brian Wilson
and Mike Love

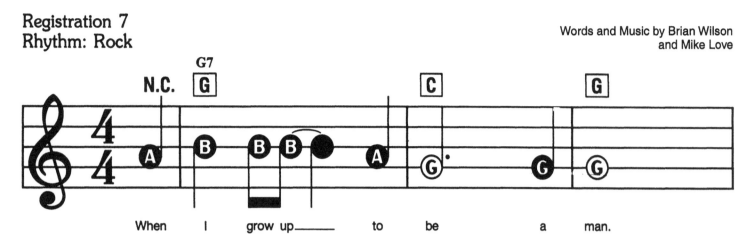

When I grow up___ to be a man.

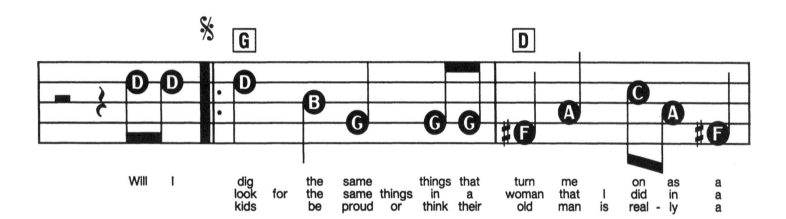

Will I dig for the same things that turn me on as a a
look for the same things in a woman that I did in a
kids be proud or think their old man is real - ly a

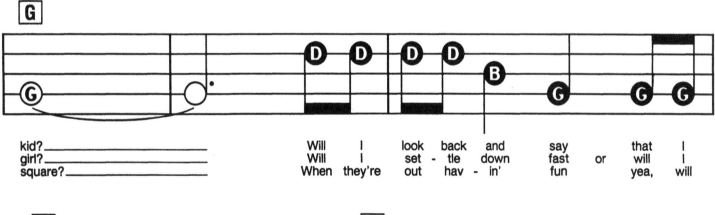

kid?___
girl?___
square?___

Will I look back and say that I
Will I set - tle down fast or will I
When they're out hav - in' fun yea, will

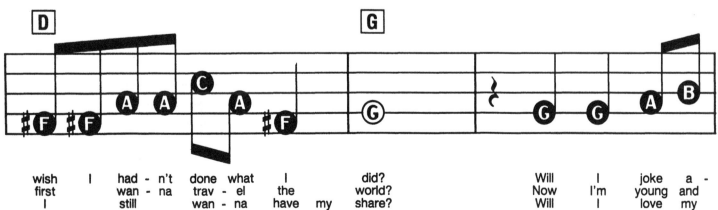

wish I had - n't done what I did?
first wan - na trav - el the world?
I still wan - na have my share?

Will I joke a -
Now I'm young and
Will I love my

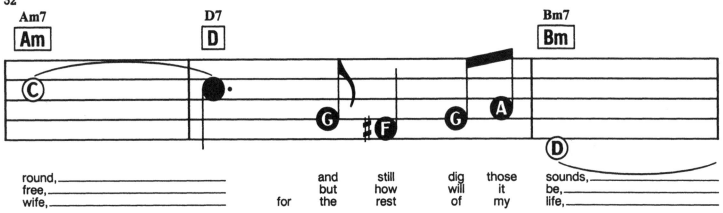

round,_____ and still dig those sounds,___
free,_____ but how will it be,___
wife,_____ for the rest of my life,___

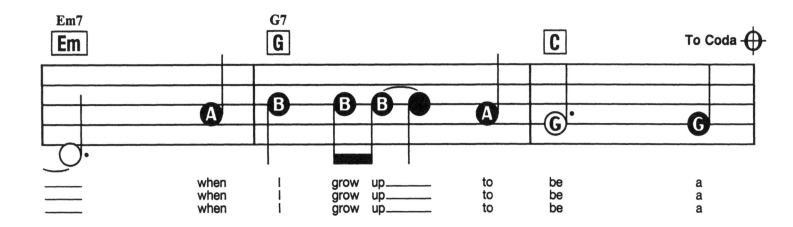

when I grow up____ to be a
when I grow up____ to be a
when I grow up____ to be a

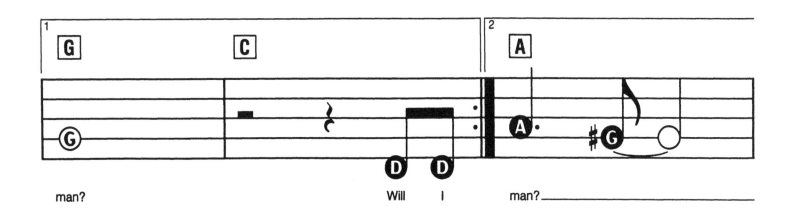

man?

Will I

man?___

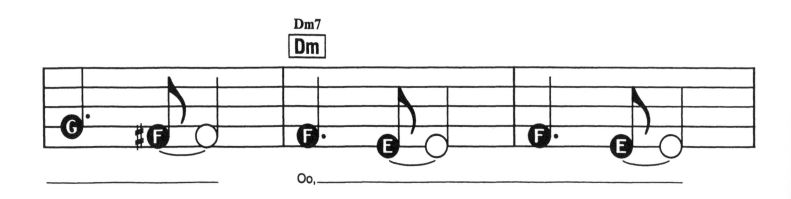

____ Oo,___

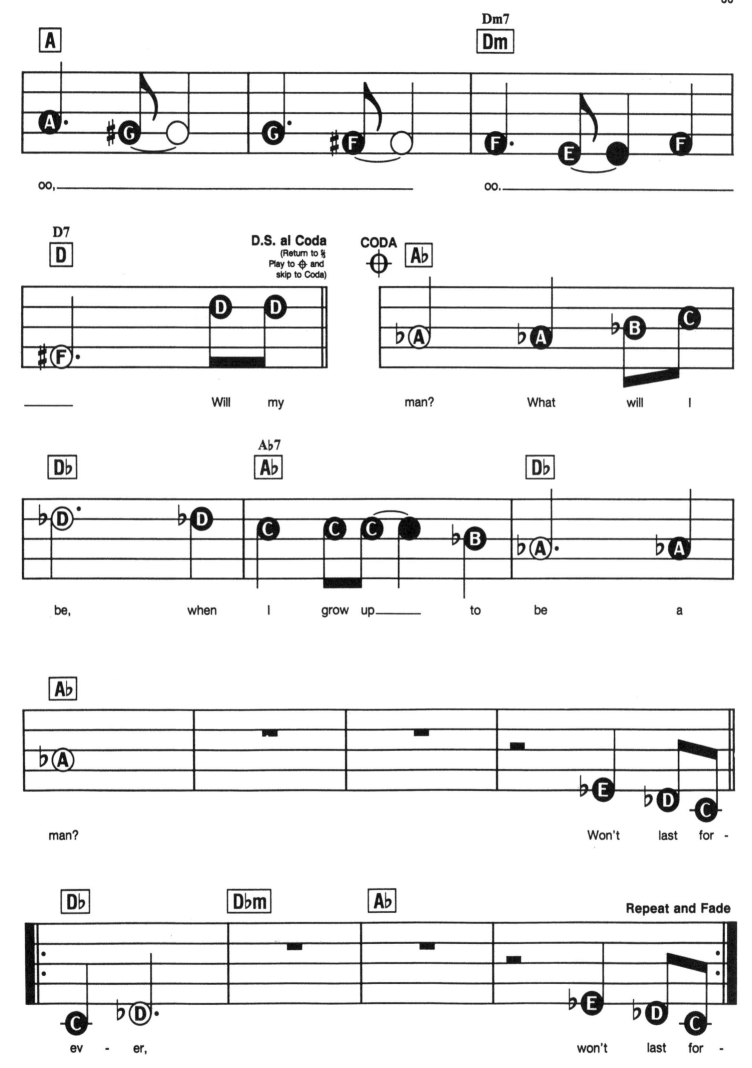

Wouldn't It Be Nice

Registration 9
Rhythm: Rock

Words and Music by Brian Wilson,
Tony Asher and Mike Love

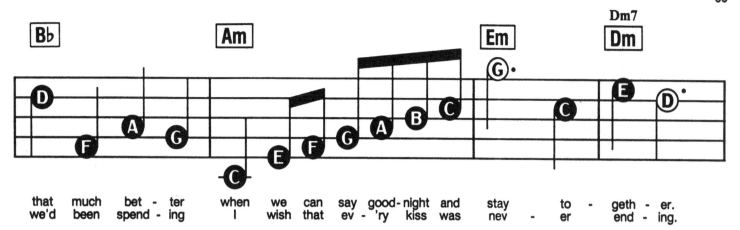

that much bet - ter when we can say good - night and stay to - geth - er.
we'd been spend - ing I wish that ev - 'ry kiss was nev - er end - ing.

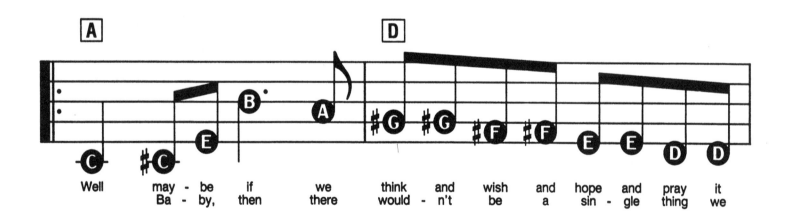

Would - n't it be

Oh, would - n't it be nice.____

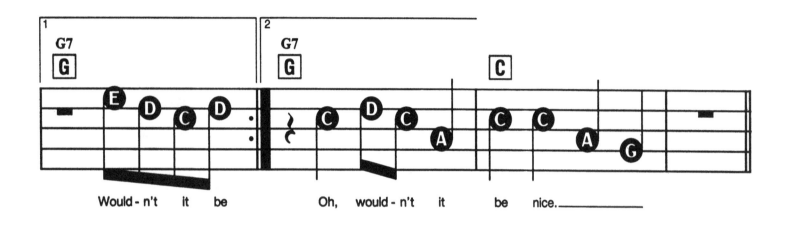

Well may - be if we think and wish and hope and pray it
Ba - by, if then we there would - n't wish be a sin - gle hope thing and we

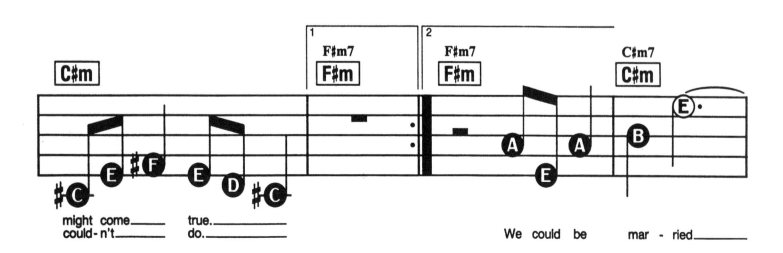

might come____ true.____
could - n't____ do.____

We could be mar - ried____

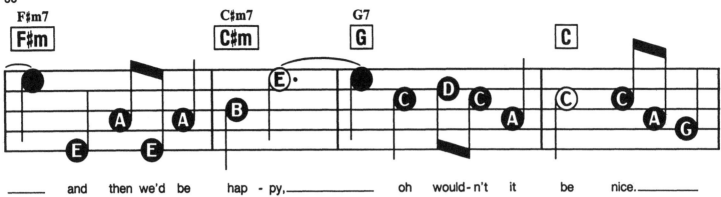

and then we'd be hap - py,_____ oh would-n't it be nice._____

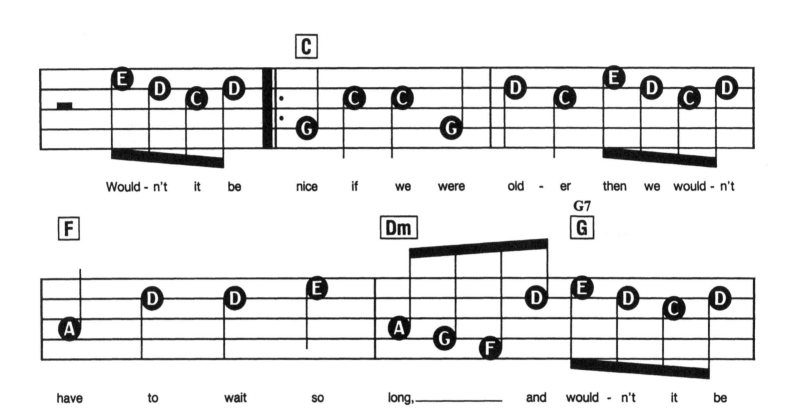

Would - n't it be nice if we were old - er then we would - n't

have to wait so long,_____ and would - n't it be

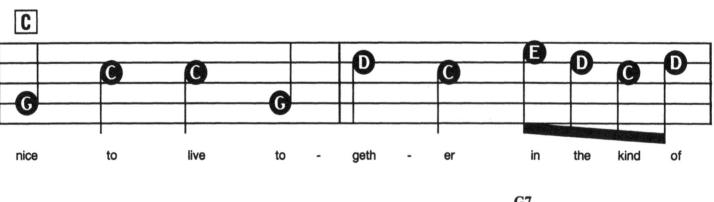

nice to live to - geth - er in the kind of

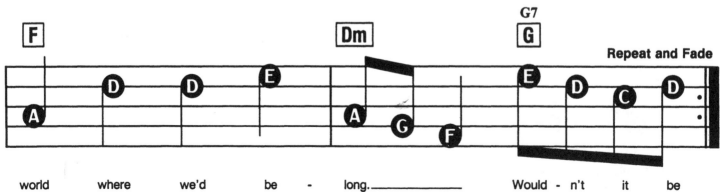

world where we'd be - long._____ Would - n't it be